How to Avoid Sexism

How to Avoid Sexism

A Guide for Writers, Editors and Publishers

Merriellyn Kett
and
Virginia Underwood

Lawrence Ragan Communications, Inc.
Chicago, Illinois

ISBN 0-931368-01-4
Manufactured in the U.S.A.

Lawrence Ragan Communications, Inc.
407 South Dearborn Street
Chicago, IL 60605

Contents

1 Sexism and the Law

We define sexism as any action, verbal or nonverbal, that assigns certain roles or characteristics to people simply on the basis of sex. Any organization that uses this particularly invidious form of stereotyping, wittingly or not, limits the aspirations and opportunities of countless women.

Sex discrimination in employment is now explicitly illegal. The Equal Pay Act of 1963 requires that women and men performing work in the same establishment under similar conditions must receive the same pay if their jobs require substantially similar skill, effort, and responsibility. All employees in all public and private institutions at all levels are covered, regardless of whether or not the institutions are receiving federal funds; however, this act covers only discrimination in salary and fringe benefits. In addition, Title VII of the Civil Rights Act of 1964 forbids discrimination on the grounds of race, color, religion, sex, or national origin in advertisements, recruitment, and on-the-job benefits. It covers salary, promotion, training, layoffs, firing, recalls, retirement policies, and the allocation of facilities. The Equal Employment Opportunity Act of 1972 extended Title VII coverage to include employees of state and local governments and employees of educational institutions. The Higher Education Act of 1972, besides extending coverage of the Equal Pay Act of 1963 to executive and administrative employees and faculty, prohibits sex discrimination in all federally assisted educational programs. Executive Order 11246, amended by Executive Order 11375, forbids discrimination in employment by all federal contractors on the basis of race, color, sex, religion, or national origin. When the Equal Rights Amendment is ratified by thirty-eight states, women will have constitutional as well as judicial and administrative protection.

Even without ERA, individual and class action suits alleging discrimination are flooding the courts, and damages are being collected. NBC has agreed to a $2 million settlement of a sex discrimination suit filed by female employees in 1975. Similar suits have cost Merrill Lynch $1.9 million and Bank of America $3 million. Northwest Airlines is fighting a court decision ordering it to pay nearly $40 million to three thousand women flight attendants. Perhaps the most widely publicized case in point was the settlement of the AT&T case in 1972. AT&T agreed to pay nearly $75 million to employees, mostly women, "whose progress may have been delayed" by previous employment practices. With this pressing motivation behind them, many employers have become anxious to avoid implying that they or their companies entertain attitudes or engage in practices which limit the advancement or full participation of their female employees.

Since sexist language in official communications can be taken as *prima facie* evidence of sexist policies and practices, employers are understandably concerned that it not appear in the memos, newsletters, and other printed materials which go out of their organization. We do not mean to suggest that "cleaning up" your language in official communications is equal to or a substitute for desexing the policies and practices of an organization, but we do think it is a valuable place to begin.

The people who must become immediately sensitized to the issues and responsive to the problems of sexism are those whose words appear in print and can be interpreted as company policy. In the final analysis this includes almost anyone in an organization. However, in practice the most vulnerable executives are those whose responsibilities include personnel and corporate communications. While the personnel department operates under explicit legal guidelines, communicators must develop their own.

This is a book about how to avoid sexism in written corporate communications. Of course sexism has legal, practical, and attitudinal ramifications as well as linguistic ones, but we will limit our attention primarily to the linguistic aspects of the problem. There are no certified experts on the subject as yet, but the need for information has developed rapidly. We will describe a number of options for avoiding sexism and let you select the one which best suits the purpose of your communication, your audience and your own style.

Editorializing

Whenever you write, you editorialize. You cannot help doing so. Words carry denotative or "dictionary" meanings and connotative or implied meanings. Writing is always an enormous challenge because these meanings are in a constant state of flux. When you write, you attempt to pin down for a moment your perception of a certain portion of reality; however, in order to communicate your perceptions, you have to use words. This does not mean that you *think* only in words or that words are even capable of exactly representing your perceptions. It does mean that in order to express what you think, you must use words.

This may seem obvious enough, but the fact that words themselves have shades of meaning attached to them can fundamentally alter the tone of what you wish to communicate. The tone becomes an integral part of your message. Even if the tone is not consciously selected, it is transmitted and is, therefore, part of the message. On top of the fact that language itself may shape the meaning of your message, the perspective of the reader or listener who receives the message will to a large extent determine which details of the message are perceived and which are filtered out. Your editorial control is determined by the extent to which you are in command of your own attitude, your choice of language and your reader's perceptions. Each of these factors is present in every communication; there is, however, wide variation in the amount of control exercised over them.

You as writer or editor have an attitude which you may not be accurately communicating. Even neutrality is an attitude. Whether this attitude is correctly and responsibly communicated will depend on the words you use as well as the other rhetorical choices you make. The language of the message may be the only thing you share directly with the reader, and the language itself has, in a sense, an attitude. Whether your own attitude is perceived as you wish will be determined by the language and rhetoric you employ as well as the attitude of your reader to your communication. For example, however vigorously you maintain that calling all executives, doctors, and citizens *he* is traditional and therefore acceptable, you increasingly run the risk that your communication will not be perceived as neutral in connotation.

Some individuals will protest that they have a positive attitude toward women and, therefore, that they cannot be called sexists. Such a person may say:

> I don't think I'm a sexist just because I naturally assume that a doctor or an executive is *he*. Most of them are. I might be surprised to find out that a particular doctor or executive was a woman, but I wouldn't be annoyed. It's just that women are more likely to be nurses or secretaries. A sexist thinks that's necessarily how the world *should be*. I don't say that. But that's how things are, and I don't think

you should try to change language until the world changes.

Those who have a very negative attitude toward women participating in the world beyond the kitchen often smugly subscribe to this reasoning, taking cover behind the assumption that language merely reflects the way the world is. The fundamental inconsistency of this position is that such a person will also refer to the average American citizen as *he*. Since 51.3% of the citizens of the United States are women, the use of *he* does not in fact reflect reality.

When the inconsistency is pointed out, the sexist will back off from the numbers explanation and will protest that the language itself is sexist. We maintain that it is always possible to avoid sexist language. No matter how honorable your intentions, if you use sexist language, you will be labelled a sexist. A significant number of people are now conscious of sexist overtones in language. These readers will perceive the writer who uses sexist language not as a good grammarian but as a sexist.

Your own neutral or positive attitude toward the legitimate aspirations of women will be distorted by your medium (that is, the language itself) and by your readers' perspectives.

2 The Generic "He"

The Perilous Pronoun

"Oh, what a beautiful baby! Is it a boy or a girl?"

This question is, of course, a breach of good taste. To call a baby an *it* is to deny the tiny person's right to human individuality. Everybody who speaks English and who has had any contact with proud parents knows this simple fact. Even if you do not share the parents' conviction that the drooling, sleepy-eyed little bundle has an individual personality, you recognize the parents' right to think so, and because you are civilized, socially responsible, and mature, you do not insult the parents and, by implication, the baby by calling it an *it*.

What can you call it then? Some people would prefer that you exclaim, "Oh, what a beautiful baby! Is *he* a boy or a girl?" However, sensitive individuals of refined judgment will usually exlaim, "Oh, what a beautiful baby! A boy or a girl?" The one thing you may be certain of from a native speaker of English is that even the most insensitive dolt around will never say, "Is *she* a boy or a girl?"

As most people are aware by now, there is a serious gap in the pronoun system of the English language. We have no third person singular pronoun which can be used without discriminating against women or offending men.

The difference in connotation between calling males *she* or excluding females with the continuous use of *he* is very real; whether the difference is described as a social or a linguistic problem, it is there, and those of us who deal in the printed word must confront it on both levels. Those who don't deal with the written language on a day to day basis encounter the problem and are forced to come up with a solution only when they encounter a very small person who is not yet adept at signalling this fundamental biological information.

Dr. Benjamin Spock is one well-known writer who has come to grips with the problem. When he first wrote his famous common-sense baby book, he noted in the preface that he would refer to the child as *he* and the parent as *she* to prevent confusion. He has since recanted this position. He says

> Like everyone else writing in the child care field, I have always referred to the baby and child with the pronouns *he* and *him.* There is a grammatical excuse, since these pronouns can be used correctly to refer to a girl or woman . . . just as the word *man* may cover women *in certain contexts.* But I now agree with the liberators of women that this is not enough of an excuse. The fact remains that this use of

> the male pronoun is one of many examples of discrimination, each of which may seem of small consequence in itself but which, when added up, help to keep women at an enormous disadvantage – in employment, in the courts, and in conventional social life.[1]

When the pronoun *he* is used to refer to a person of indeterminate sex, the grammatical justification is that *he* is being used generically. The eighteenth-century grammarians who prescribed *he* to cover both *he* and *she* were borrowing the usage from the then current common law practice of coverture. This doctrine depends upon the assumption that women are inferior to men, and therefore in need of male protection. It was articulated by the influential jurist, William Blackstone. Consider the following discussion of the disposition of women's property rights in both England and the Colonies.

> By marriage, the husband and wife are one person in law; that is, the very being or legal existence of the woman is suspended during the marriage, or at least is incorporated and consolidated into that of the husband, under whose wing, protection, and cover, she performs everything. For this reason, a man cannot grant anything to his wife, or enter into covenant with her, for the grant would be to suppose her separate existence. . . .[2]

In the past, therefore, the generic *he* was not only grammatically correct but legally precise as well. Legally speaking a woman's existence as an individual ceased on her wedding day, and this view of women as weak, helpless, infantile, and incomplete without a male protector haunts women to this day.

In the past a businesswoman was forced to accept the discrimination against her implicit in the generic *he* as coming with the territory she was knowingly invading. As a practical matter it seemed quite natural that those to whom she was not personally known in the business world would assume that she was male. It was even supposed to be the highest compliment to a woman if her work were considered "as good as any man's."

We are in a transition stage now. More and more women are invading and surviving in what was formerly and unquestionably a man's world. In this transition stage, if you guess that a business person you don't know is a man, you will still be right more often than you are wrong. Nevertheless, however much you welcome or deplore it, the future is near, and in the future the chances that an unknown person may be either male or female will be equal to the proportion of males to females in the general population.

In the future it will become as socially unacceptable to call an unknown business executive *he* as it currently is to call a baby you've not met before an *it*. In the future we can safely predict that social pressure will de-sex the language, and the avoidance of unintended insults will become as automatic as the public avoidance of racial and ethnic slurs is now. At the present time, however, the language is lagging. Even those writers who sincerely wish to avoid blatantly sexist language find themselves unsure about the proper choice of a third person singular pronoun. Those who must write business letters and other official communications may find themselves stumbling about in the language they have been using effectively and responsibly for years. Choosing the right pronoun is a problem not only when you bend over a baby carriage but daily.

If you wish to write a memo, for example, about the responsibilities of a sales manager, an editor, a teacher, a representative of your company in any capacity, you learned long ago that you may say *he* and every sales manager, editor, teacher, or representative who is not a *he* will know that *she* must share the responsibilities under discussion. However, an increasing number of women and men object to this usage. If your primary purpose is to communicate their responsibilities, it makes good sense from a rhetorical point of view not to alienate your readers or distract their attention from your message.

If you are comfortable with the convention, you probably feel annoyed and put upon that women should start demanding equality of treatment from pronouns when so many other issues of so much greater importance await solution. There is a good reason why women are finding it increasingly difficult to accept the exclusion implicit in the unrelieved use of the generic *he,* however. The Westside Women's Committee puts it this way:

> When we constantly personify the judge, the critic, the executive, the author, the artist, the politician, the leader, the candidate, etc. as male by using the pronoun *he* we are subtly conditioning ourselves

> *against* the idea of a female writer, judge, critic, executive, politician or candidate. We are programming ourselves not to *expect* a female in these roles, and we are therefore less prepared to *accept* a female in these roles. This process thus denies them equal encouragement to pursue certain roles, and reinforces prejudiced evaluation of them when they do pursue such roles.[3]

The Committee also points out that another result is that the usage distorts our conceptualization and consequently the proposed solutions for the social problems of, for example, the juvenile run-away, the diabetic, and the septugenarian. We tend to lose sight of the fact that most of these individuals are female when we refer to one of them with the pronoun *he*.

Consider the statement made by Albert Bleumenthal, a New York State Assemblyman, who in 1975 during debate on the abortion issue came out with the decided opinion that "everyone should be able to decide for *himself* whether or not to have an abortion." What on Earth could he have meant? Is it the generic use of *himself?* Or does he mean that the husband, father, or boyfriend of the pregnant woman has the right to decide for himself whether or not the woman may have an abortion? If Mr. Bleumenthal did not mean to imply this, if he were only obeying the conventional rules of traditional grammar, then his statement is merely ridiculous.

To deny that it is extraordinarily difficult to write an extended piece of prose without invoking the prescribed "neutral" or generic pronoun is to seriously underestimate the perils awaiting the mildly conscientious communicator who sets out to write in completely nonsexist prose. It is easy enough to avoid the third person singular personal pronoun in a sentence or two, but the stylistic contortions and distortions which may result can become grotesque after a paragraph or so if you have only one technique in your repertoire.

Since this book is addressed for the most part to people who are interested in good writing as well as in avoiding sexism, it shouldn't be necessary to underrate the problem by implying that if *you* find it difficult to adapt yourself to nonsexist pronouns, you are a closet male chauvinist regardless of your sex or your professed good intentions.

In editing for sexism, as in any copy-editing whether you're working with your own writing or that of someone else, the natural impulse is to change the fewest possible number of words. Recasting a sentence is always troublesome, and in recasting you can easily shift the desired emphasis so that you may end up having to go back and recast an entire paragraph or even an entire article or memorandum to get rid of sexist undercurrents.

Avoiding the generic *he* involves a conscious interruption of habitual forms of expression. It involves censoring the carefully trained intuition upon which you as a professional language user have come to rely. Many reasonable and sympathetic writers and editors, both male and female, who are anxious to get rid of implied slurs in all other aspects of their work balk when it comes to the pronoun.

Let's take a look at some of your alternatives and discuss each from a stylistic point of view.

Common gender pronouns: an unlikely solution

To many writers the most obvious thing to do is to invent a pronoun to fill the gap in the language, and a good number of people have come forward with suggestions. This would be very handy for the copy-editor or the communicator charged with seeing that no blatantly sexist language appears in official organizational communications. All you would need to do is replace *he* with the substitute pronoun which would be defined as singular and indiscriminately masculine or feminine.

In 1973 students at the University of Tennessee decided to try out a set of common gender pronouns, *tey* (nominative), *ter* (possessive), and *tem* (objective), in the student newspaper, *The Daily Beacon*. Although scheduled to last for eight months, the experiment was dropped after only three. Casey Miller and Kate Swift discuss the *Beacon's* experiment in their book *Words and Women*. They quote an example from the paper's policy statement indicating the appropriate use of the new set of pronouns.

> A new *chancellor* will be appointed in late summer, but *tey* will take office in the fall after the University has given *tem* time to learn *ter* responsibilities.[4]

Ironically a member of the University's English Department complained about the "poor raped pronouns." The use of the word *rape* is thought-provoking in this context. It not too subtly reminds the reader who the victims of rape are supposed to be, suggesting that tampering with the pronouns is tantamount to upsetting the natural order of things. One's perception of what is logical and "right" in Nature and in society is often a function of what is conventionally expressed through the syntax and semantics of a particular language. Can one avoid the question of whether this individual actually meant to imply, as a logical unwinding of the metaphor compels us to think, that just as men are not the victims of rape, women are not chancellors? It cannot be denied that to refer to the University's as-yet-unappointed chancellor as *he* and *him* and to refer to *his* responsibilities unavoidably suggests that this individual will, in fact *must*, be a man. Some writers regularly resort to sexual images in linguistic discussions ("Our language is being emasculated"; "My text was sterilized"). If this weren't so funny, it would be quite sad.

The number of substitutes for the generic *he* which have been proposed over the years should by itself indicate the difficulty with this proposal. In order for a substitute to work, people have got to use it, which means that a lot of people have got not only to agree that a new pronoun is needed, but they have got to agree on just what the word is to be. The virulent response to *tey, ter, tem* makes it obvious that this set of pronouns was not destined for wide public acceptance.

The most successful of the recommended gap-fillers so far has probably been the word *co* suggested by Mary

Orovan in a 1970 article entitled "Humanizing English."[5] The new pronoun is used routinely in a magazine called *Communities* which serves cooperative-living groups across the country, and it is reported to have spread into a number of these alternative-life-style communities. Consider the problems involved in editing a memo which read:

> The *sales manager* should make certain that *he* lets no sexist slurs enter into any of the routine sales presentations of *his* salesmen.

This could be changed quickly and easily to:

> The *sales manager* should make certain that *co* lets no sexist slurs enter into the routine sales presentations of *co* salespeople.

Try substituting the suggested pronoun *co* into a couple of the following sentences for yourself. Do it as openmindedly and as conscientiously as you can:

> A motorist planning a trip must make a series of decisions. _______ must select a route of travel. _______ must decide upon a time of departure and arrival. _______ must determine how many hours _______ wishes to drive.

Now we are going to give you some fairly exciting news. Life has been discovered on Mars, and a team of anthropologists has set forth to study the creature they've found. It is called a *gwangle*. Fill in the name of the new discovery as you read through the next few sentences:

> The ______ is the only known form of animal life on Mars. ______ live to be several thousand years old. A ______ fur is green, and it has pointed ears. The ______ is bisexual and performs which ever sexual function appeals to it at the moment. ______ have not been able to comprehend the term *sexism*, though they have expressed interest in the other social customs of Earthlings.

Although both of the preceding short passages are syntactically very simple, as a reader and speaker of English you are much more likely to accept the word *gwangle* than *co*. This is true in spite of the fact that you are well aware that both men and women drive cars and in spite of the fact that you seriously question whether there really is a Martian creature called a *gwangle*. You will even accept *gwangle* in spite of the fact that the *g-w* combination is not one that you would normally use in English. (Can you think of a single word that begins with *g-w*?) And in spite of the fact that *co* is a familiar sound (appearing in words like *copilot* and *colon)* and in spite of the fact that *co* is intrinsically meaningful (*co* words often indicate a combining of two things), it is distinctly more difficult to read through the first passage making the substitutions than it is to read through the second even while automatically changing from the singular to the plural to the possessive forms as required by the syntax.

What is it about the pronoun that makes it more difficult to manipulate? Pronouns are *function* or *structure* words. The four major parts of speech are nouns, verbs, adjectives, and adverbs. All other kinds of words are called function words because they signal the function of the major parts of speech in a sentence. The language takes in new nouns with considerable ease (note *gwangle*), and picks up verbs, adjectives, and adverbs as the need is felt, but new function words are rarely added. There are only a few hundred such words in the language altogether, and compared to the approximately one hundred thousand words that an educated person may recognize, that really is not very many. The function words are enormously stable, however, and although they are few in number, they are used far more frequently than the most common nouns and verbs. According to a recent study,[6] the ten most common words used in written English are *the, of, and, to, a, in, that, is, was* and *he.* (*She,* by the way, shows up as number thirty-seven in this study.) Except for *is* and *was*, which are traditionally labelled as verbs, all of the others are unequivocally function words.

The number of publishers' guidelines to their writers and editors on avoiding sexism which we have reviewed are uniformly silent about the possibility of the creation of a common gender singular pronoun to replace *he*. Let's assume that future attitudes toward the creation of a new pronoun will continue to meet with strong resistance, and let's consider the other syntactic options open to us.

He or she: use compounding sparingly

A second solution, the substitution of *he or she* or *he/she* for *he*, is certainly ridiculous if overused or inconsistently used. Nevertheless, a single sentence using *he or she* is a workable option and should be in your repertoire of solutions for avoiding sexism.

> As a *child* matures, *he or she* will be eager to take on new responsibilities.

There would be nothing stylistically objectionable about this sentence if it appeared, for example, as a caption on a picture. However, on a stylistic level, there are two things wrong with the continued use of *he or she*, and both have the same result: they make the serious attempt to avoid sexist language look ridiculous. This automatic reflex action, the ridiculing of every feminine attempt to become incorporated into the more serious aspects of life, is part of what a conscientious communicator wants to avoid.

Consider the following attempt by an individual writing on popular culture to eliminate sexism from an article:

> If television is substituted for a babysitter – that is, the *child* is simply placed in front of the set while the parents ignore *him/her* – television becomes a major source of information about the reality of that particular home and/or society. In a sense, television becomes one of the "significant others," albeit an electronic one, from which the *child* gains information about *his* world.[7]

As you can see, the greatest danger with trying to simply repeat *he or she* (or *he/she*), *him or her* (or *him/her*) is that you will give up half-way through the sentence and revert to the generic *he* as this writer has done.

Inconsistency in the use of the *he or she* solution will convince the reader that your attempt to avoid sexism is hypocritical at best, and from a stylistic point of view it is obviously much to be preferred that the writer never begin the compounding than to abandon it half-way through a single sentence. Equally objectionable to most of those who are at best only ambivalently committed to avoiding sexism is to carry out the compounding to ridiculous lengths.

> *He or she* will not know what is expected of *him or her* unless *he or she* has had an opportunity to work through the routine with *his or her* partner and then has repeated the procedure by *himself or herself.*

For anyone to suggest that a literate feminist would advocate the continuation of that sort of syntax is nonsense. Without the feminine addenda this is a perfectly ordinary, somewhat pedantic sentence of English. With the feminine pronouns it is neither ordinary, pedantic, nor English. Compounding the pronouns can be used as a technique for avoiding sexism, but it must be used sparingly. You should seriously reconsider any paragraph which invokes the compounding privilege more than once or twice.

Compounding also becomes a problem when you start out with *men and women*, as the writer of the following advertising material for a brokerage house did, but then abandon the *women* and use exclusively masculine pronouns:

> On Wall Street, the image of the account executive defies simple definition. To some he is a *salesman* or, in Street vernacular, a customer's *man*. To others, *he* is a link between the analyst and client, and a communicator/consultant as well. To still others, *he* is looked upon as a semi-independent *businessman* who is somehow one step removed from the firm *he* represents.
>
> This latter definition is the only one that decidedly does not apply to the *men and women* who are Oppenheimer's principal source of contact with its clients. The Oppenheimer account executive is a valued associate whose pride in *his* firm is a mirror image of *his* pride in *himself*.
>
> . . . Instead, as noted earlier, we expect each account executive to be in frequent contact with any or all of our analysts who can provide *him* with the facts *he* must have to be of meaningful service to *his* clients.[8]

Quite obviously the writer believes that the average account executive is male. Even if this was true when the literature was written, it will not necessarily be true in the future. The passage is a flaming example of sex role stereotyping. You'll notice that *clients* is always carefully pluralized. Anyone with money, regardless of sex, is welcome to become a client of Oppenheimer. However, are only men welcome to apply for the position of account executive? This is almost certainly not true, although that is what this writer has said by connotation.

We would by no means advocate writing a sentence like,

> The Oppenheimer account *executive* is a valued associate whose pride in *his or her* firm is a mirror image of *his or her* pride in *himself or herself*.

However, if Oppenheimer willingly employs both *men and women*, the inappropriate exclusion of their female executives could be avoided as easily as the exclusion of female clients was by pluralizing.

> Oppenheimer account *executives* are valued associates whose pride in *their* firm is a mirror image of *their* pride in *themselves.*

Pluralize to avoid vast abstractions: the typical human being is not male

> Progress has been made in our equal opportunity posture through our collective efforts in recent years, but much still needs to be accomplished. . . . *Each member* of Management, along with *his* other objectives and goals, will be held accountable for carrying out the Affirmative Action Program in *his* area of responsibility. . . .

Incredible though it may be, this sentence actually appears in a corporate policy statement which outlines in detail the organization's Affirmative Action policy. Could you blame a female employee of this company for thinking that its management is not as committed to equal opportunity as they protest? One of the easiest and most productive solutions for avoiding the problem of the generic *he* is to pluralize the word to which *he* (*his, him*) refers and convert the pronoun to *they* (*their, them*).

> *All members* of Management, along with *their* other objectives and goals, will be held accountable for carrying out the Affirmative Action Program in *their* areas of responsibility.

This is possible because in English the third person singular pronouns (*he, she,* and *it*) are the only ones which have gender. This is a characteristic of the language which has survived from Old English. The third person plural pronouns (*they, their, them*) are and always have been common gender, just like *you* and *we*, but unlike the French *ils* for the masculine and *elles* for the feminine plural.

Although as speakers of English we are used to thinking of our language, particularly the function or structure words, as reflections of the laws of nature, there is little to support the belief. In Old English, for example, the second person pronouns had both singular and plural forms, but the singular *thee, thou, thine* virtually disappeared in Modern English, although many Southerners in the United States still feel a distinction between *you* and the plural *you all* is desirable.

Historically, English, like its sister language German, marked gender in an arbitrary fashion on its nouns. *Wife* was neuter; *stone* was masculine; *shovel* was feminine. Gender is a linguistic term which, as you can tell from these examples, has nothing to do with sex. At least gender has nothing to do with sex in languages which use gender distinctions. The only gender marking we now use in English is, according to grammarians, "natural" gender.

This means *it* is used for inanimate objects; *she* is used for everything clearly female (or beautiful like a ship, or cantankerous like a car, or small like a cat); and *he* applies to everything else. Feminists argue that the "everything else" has operated in the past to exclude women from "everything else" except exclusively female, which is to say sexual, roles.

The so-called "generic" *he* has persisted, in our opinion, precisely because through socialization native speakers of American English have learned to assign masculine gender to nouns which describe important functions in society. *Doctor, lawyer, repairman, engineer, policeman,* and *senator* were all considered masculine nouns, as were *taxpayer* and *citizen* because children have learned early that the contributions of women are economically and politically inconsequential. It is inaccurate to suggest that there is something "natural" about doctors and taxpayers being *he.* If you persist in the use of generic *he* to refer to the typical doctor or taxpayer, the unavoidable connotation is that you consider these nouns to have masculine rather than common gender.

Our spoken language shows a greater need for a common gender singular pronoun than it does for a singular/plural distinction. That is why we hear "*Everybody* did what *they* could" and "*The average person* will do what *they* can to help if *they* recognize that an emergency exists" and "whether *a teacher* can really teach or not, *they* are usually respected." These sentences are, according to the reactionary rules of grammar we inherited from the eighteenth century, ungrammatical; nonetheless, it is clear that adopting the common gender plural pronoun when a common gender singular noun is the antecedent is what the language itself wants to do.

The average person is not a *he.* If you say, "The average *person* will do what *he* can to help if *he* recognizes that an emergency exists," whether it is your intention or not, you perpetuate the demeaning and inaccurate assumption that in an emergency a man will rise to the occasion while a woman will either fall apart or stand by helplessly.

Consider the following passage from *Engineering Education News:*

> What kind of person engages in continuing education? What motivates them? How is their job performance affected? This new book from ASEE investigates these questions to provide insight into the need for continuing education for the practicing engineer and benefits gained.[9]

This passage has a great deal to recommend it. It is part of a very brief review of a book which will be of interest to engineers, employers, and professional educators interested in continuing education. It is to the point, succinct, nonsexist, but it is incorrect according to textbook grammar. We have every reason to believe that using *they, their,* and *them* to refer to singular antecedents like *person* will eventually be an accepted solution to the rejection of *he* as a common gender singular pronoun. It is a solution which has considerably greater odds of catching on than a new made-up pronoun; it is already widely used in speech and often in informal writing. If you use the construction in speech, you will be in very respectable company. Walter Cronkite uses it, as do many well-educated and respected people when they are speaking unself-consciously. William Shakespeare advised "everyone to rest themselves," and George Bernard Shaw said, "It's enough to drive anyone out of their senses." Scott Fitzgerald who was in constant competitive conflict with his wife Zelda said candidly that "Nobody likes a mind quicker than their own." And John F. Kennedy observed, "If that person gets sick, they are in the hospital for more than two weeks."

It should be carefully understood that these quotations are not meant to demonstrate that the speakers were being ungrammatical. What is grammatical in formal situations is defined as that which is used by the most well-educated and well-respected writers. Surely these gentlemen qualify. Unfortunately many copy-editors much prefer to trust their outmoded grammar books than the actual language of even the most prestigious speakers and writers. They forget that languages change to meet changing social conditions and the whims and preferences of language users. If it didn't, we would probably be speaking some ancient form of Sanskrit.

The extraordinary thing which is happening now is that a large number of people who use a particular language, English, have decided to change the language in a very fundamental way, but we are saddled with a general attitude toward language which makes tampering with what is considered linguistically "right" and "wrong" tantamount to blasphemy or rape, as the English department faculty member at the University of Tennessee complained.

For now, until some official organization such as the Modern Language Association or the National Council of Teachers of English legitimizes the standard spoken use of *they* as a singular, nonsexist substitute for *he*, you may feel more comfortable avoiding the usage altogether. The best thing to do is probably to pluralize the "typical person" to whom the pronoun refers.

If you ask, "What kind of person engages in continuing education?" you are in effect asserting that a portrait of the typical person can be drawn. If your statistics show that the typical person is female, a significant piece of information is disguised by the use of the pronoun *he*. If there is no significant difference between the number of males and the number of females whom the "typical" description is meant to cover, it is equally misleading to suggest that the typical person is male. If the typical person *is* male, the use of *he* tends to suggest that the occasional woman who is included under the description is abnormal in an extremely unflattering sense. It has been suggested that under this sort of negative psychological pressure, only a woman who was a superstar in terms of talent and intellect or one who was already seriously neurotic could afford to succeed in a "man's" profession. Avoiding *he*, while it will not remove all the obstacles in a woman's path as she struggles to gain access to a formerly all-male position, is equal to taking down the "whites only" sign in a restaurant. She may still get seated by the kitchen and have the soup spilled on her, but at least she is inside the door.

From a stylistic point of view, in order to avoid the officially ungrammatical use of *they* to refer back to a singular referent (the typical *engineer*), in very formal writing the thing to do is to pluralize the referent (*engineers*). If you are writing from scratch, you should be on the lookout for the singular noun whose function is to describe the "typical" person, then pluralize it on the spot because the pronoun *he* will be attracted to it like fleas to a dog. Trying to pick them out of a memo which has already been typed or an article which has already been set in print will be as frustrating as it is expensive. In situations which can in any way be construed to be informal, the *everyone/they* or the *typical person engaged in continuing eduction/they* construction will pass as ordinary standard English. To "correct" the *they* is inaccurate, misleading, pedantic, and sexist. It does not increase precision in meaning but actively decreases it. However in formal situations where you decide to pluralize the troublesome antecedent and switch the generic *he* to the plural *they*, always double-check the rest of the sentence for agreement. Look closely at the following passage:

> The *applicants* should not mark in *their* test booklet, and *they* should use a computer answer sheet for easy scoring.

It is improbable that all of the applicants will have the same test booklet or that they will all use a single computer sheet. Although it is highly unlikely that you would make this sort of mistake if you were actually writing in the plural, the problem can creep in unawares when you are editing. The longer the edited passage is, of course, the greater the danger that an agreement problem will slip in. In editing for sexism you will tend to focus on one feature at a time, and you may ignore the impact on the rest of the passage. When this happens, the tone becomes either immature or ridiculous. It happens not because careless editing for sexism inevitably leads to ridiculous sounding syntax, but because careless editing for any single feature can lead to very unnatural sounding syntax. If you cut your foot while chopping wood, you don't blame the ax; nor should you conclude that editing for sexism is an impossible task if you make an occasional goof.

The following foolish sounding sentence was produced by an editor for a publishing company ostensibly committed to the avoidance of sexism:

> I believe that the preface pretends to address itself to the *student* but will lose *him or her* and may strike *him* as your effort to sound like you're with *him* at the same time that you are really selling out to the instructor.

It could have easily been written with a plural noun in the first place:

> I believe that the preface pretends to address itself to the *students* but will lose *them* and may strike *them* as your effort to sound like you're with *them* at the same time that you are really selling out to the instructor.

The trick, of course, is to catch the singular noun which means "the typical student," "the typical engineer," or "the typical editor" before you write it. The sooner you catch the expression, the sooner you will start thinking and hence writing in the plural, and the fewer unintentional agreement mistakes you will make. A useful byproduct may be an increased awareness that "the typical anything" is a seriously over-simplified concept. If the typical person is not male, then you must broaden your thinking as well as your writing.

Beware the indefinite pronoun: it leads to *he*

An obvious rhetorical extension of "the typical person" discussed in the last section is the frequent use of indefinite pronouns like *everyone, someone, anyone, everybody, somebody, anybody, one, another, no one,* and *nobody.* Indefinite pronouns are those psychologically plural but grammatically singular words which beguile you into thinking you've included *everyone* then half-way through the sentence force you into the masculine *he* for a referent.

Offering advice on the indefinite pronouns is a delicate and dangerous task because of everyone's differing notions of what is standard English and what is not. It should be very clear to anyone who listens with half an ear that, "Everyone took off their coats," is a very natural sentence to hear from speakers with impeccable academic and social credentials. Virginia McDavid and Macklin Thomas in their text *Basic Writing* (1974) call the indefinite pronouns "psychologically plural" and suggest changing the sentence in formal writing to the plural form; the *Prentice-Hall Handbook for Writers* (1974) calls the distinction formal versus informal. *The Random House Handbook* (1974) calls the necessity of using the masculine personal pronouns after the indefinite pronouns, "a legitimate matter of complaint," then adds, "but as yet no substitute form has been widely adopted."

The National Council of Teachers of English maintains that, "In all but strictly formal usage, plural pronouns have become acceptable substitutes for the masculine singular," following an indefinite pronoun. Unfortunately, the NCTE does not define what exactly "formal usage" is. In browsing through the journals of the NCTE since the publication of their "Guidelines for Nonsexist Use of Language in NCTE Publications" we have not been able to find an example of an indefinite pronoun followed by either a form of *he* or a form of *they*. Perhaps we have not looked closely enough, or, more likely, the construction is being scrupulously avoided. We did find the following candid introduction to a Guest Editorial in the *English Journal*. It was written by Dwight L. Burton, a former Editor of the NCTE journal:

> Myth, or whatever, has it that as you grow older (I'd use "one grows" here except for the problem of the next pronoun resulting from the sexist flap) you grow more conservative and more mellow.[10]

The difference between "as you grow older" and "as one grows older" is one of tone. The indefinite pronouns add a touch of formality; if you use them you assume a somewhat elevated, almost omniscient stance. You look out over the landscape, observe, and generalize. On the other hand, when you address the reader directly, you say, "This is the way it was with me, and I expect it'll be this way for you too." The tone is more informal, more personal. In this case, the informal tone of the Editorial is established first by the use of *you* and is reinforced by the irreverent tone of the parenthetical comment on the choice of *you* which is used to establish the truth of the statement that "as you grow older, you grow more conservative and more mellow."

Young or old, everyone is more conservative about their language than any other aspect of their lives. Eventually *they, their*, and *them* will become generally acceptable as common gender singular pronoun referents; in the meantime, the English profession's resistance to the sexist use of *he, his,* and *him* to refer to *everyone* seems to be passive resistance, avoiding the troublesome constructions entirely.

The traditional explanation for using the singular *he* after the indefinite pronouns has been that *everyone* refers to all people but that it refers to them one at a time. "Everyone took their seat," is considered imprecise because, it is argued, everyone did not sit down together in one large chair. If you say, "Everyone took his seat," it is clear that everyone who sat down sat down one at a time in a separate chair.

This explanation would be as good as any if it didn't trouble you that, everything else being equal, 51.3% of the people referred to were not male. From a strictly logical point of view, then, it would make sense to argue that it would be safer to assume that *everyone* had a chair of *their* own than that *everyone* was a *he*. The explanation is clearly spurious if you say, "Everyone took off their coats," where the plural *coats* removes the possibility that everyone arrived wrapped together in one large overcoat.

Traditional grammatical explanations are not logical; they are made up after a convention has been established to help people who have not yet learned the convention to remember it. If the convention were an expression of natural logic, everyone who speaks the language would acquire it automatically and know it intuitively, and no explanation would be necessary. For example, it is not felt necessary to explain word order in English sentences. The subject comes in front of the verb and the object follows it because that's the way English is. On the other hand, languages which do not use the subject/verb/object word order are never considered abnormal by those who speak them.

Frederick Crews in *The Random House Handbook* concludes his discussion of the problem of indefinite pronouns by saying:

> *His* is still regarded as "common gender," with the somewhat cumbersome *his or her* available for times when you want to indicate unmistakably that both sexes are intended.

His statement recognizes that females are excluded by the generic *he*, but he shrugs his shoulders at the whole problem. We suspect Mr. Crews would argue that the choice of a pronoun is a trivial problem, but we would like to suggest that you advertise yourself, your attitudes, and the attitudes of the company you work for whenever you put your pen to paper. It seems to us that Mr. Crews is condoning the exclusion of women. Our conviction is reinforced by a sentence in his discussion of faulty syntax. The problem sentence, which appears on the same page with his dismissal of the generic *he* issue, reads:

> Roberta is an efficient worker who, if you wanted to employ *her*, would spare you an ugly lawsuit.

Roberta might best be hired, he appears to us to say, not because she is an efficient worker but because of the ugly lawsuit she might initiate if she is discriminated against. Nasty, querulous, unladylike Roberta. When the exclusion of women is legally inexpedient, even Mr. Crews would recommend avoiding the generic *he.*

The syntax of the usual English sentence which includes an indefinite pronoun will inevitably force a confrontation with the generic singular pronoun.

> A conservative is *someone* who can endure the suffering of others for the sake of *his* own principles.

This sentence tends to suggest that a woman would not be a conservative. Basically, there are four ways to solve this problem. One way you can avoid suggesting that all conservatives are men is by rephrasing the sentence with *you* instead of *someone:*

> *You* are a *conservative* if *you* can endure the suffering of others for the sake of *your* own principles.

This solution adds a more personal, informal tone to your prose which we do not consider inappropriate, and it may cause your audience to read it more carefully.

In informal situations, you may select the second strategy, using *they, their,* and *them* as pronoun referents.

> A *conservative* is *someone* who can endure the suffering of others for the sake of *their* own principles.

Traditionally, however, this sentence will be construed to read that the principles under discussion are those of the sufferers, in which case what is being defined is a martyr and not a conservative. If you wish to be in the vanguard with the use of this solution, make sure that your antecedent is unmistakable and be prepared for a fair degree of contempt from the linguistically conservative. They will lose, but it may be awhile yet.

Your third option is to pluralize the referent:

> *Conservatives* are those who can endure the suffering of others for the sake of *their* own principles.

A fourth solution following the indefinite pronoun is to omit the *his* entirely or change it to an article adjective (*a, an, the*).

> A conservative is *someone* who can endure the suffering of others for the sake of principle.
>
> or
>
> for the sake of *a* principle.

This is in many ways the happiest of the solutions we have proposed, so long as the next sentence does not start with *he*. As we noticed when we discussed *he or she* as a substitute for the generic *he*, if you abandon your solution half way through the passage, the problem itself still remains.

Because English syntax seems to conspire against their nonsexist good intentions, many people give it one good conscientious effort and then conclude that avoiding sexism in a thoroughly sexist language is impossible. In order to succeed, you will need more than good intentions, more even than a commitment; you need a number of alternatives in your repertoire, and you need to juggle the alternatives around until you find the right one for what you are trying to communicate. The way you use language is habitual, not necessary. To argue that it is necessary to imply in writing that *everyone* is *he* is like arguing that smoking cigarettes is necessary for good respiration. It may be a difficult habit to break, but it is not a necessary one.

The "generic" *she*: an unworkable alternative

Some of you may have been really put off by working with unfamiliar common gender pronouns like *co* and *tey* and may even have come to feel that the generic *he* problem is a trivial one. Many people, men particularly, feel this way and claim that they're ready and willing to address the issue of sexism in a sporting fashion as long as they don't have to use ridiculous new words.

Columnist Gena Corea has offered this individual an interesting solution. Since more women than men think the problem needs attention, she suggests replacing the generic *he* with the generic *she*. Her reasoning goes like this:

> If women think it's important and men don't . . . let's use a pronoun that pleases women. Men don't care what it is as long as it's not clumsy so, from now on, let's use *she* to refer to the standard human being. The word *she* includes *he* so that would be fair. Anyway, we've used *he* for the past several thousand years and we'll use *she* for the next thousand; we're just taking turns."[11]

Try substituting the generic *she* into a couple of sentences for yourself:

> Every executive must select a leadership pattern. ________ usually has some freedom in choice of leadership styles, so ________ must decide which of ________ leadership options is best in dealing with ________ subordinates.

Satisfying as the above substitution experience may have been for women, we cannot seriously recommend this solution. The generic *she* is fraught with the same problems as the generic *he.* As an exercise, however, it may have been particularly instructive for male readers. It should make it easier for them to empathize with the female executive (doctor, astronaut, mail carrier, welder) who is sick of being referred to as *he*.

Notice that removing sexism from language has important consequences for how we interpret the motivation of women in formerly male-dominated occupations. Many men ridicule the woman who wants to be a welder, a doctor, or an editor for "wanting to be a man." Linguistic convention encourages us to refer to doctors and welders as *he*, but the doctor or welder who happens to be a woman probably does not want to be a man or to be called a man; what she probably wants is the money (a thoroughly red-blooded American motivation) that goes with the job. Or she may like working with her hands. Or she may like fighting disease. Wanting to be a doctor is not the same thing as wanting to be a man. In the Soviet Union, for example, where caring for the sick is not a means of acquiring wealth, some seventy-five percent of the M.D.s are women, although the more prestigious medical research positions still tend to be dominated by men.

Ursula Le Guin has provided some remarkable insight into not only the use of pronouns but the entire question of sex roles in society. In her novel *The Left Hand of Darkness* (1969) she refers, much to the consternation of some feminists, to the androgynous inhabitants of the planet Winter as *he*. To redress the grievance somewhat, in a 1975 version of her short story, "Winter's King," about the same planet of androgynes, she adopts the feminine pronoun, the "generic" *she*, though she preserves the masculine titles King and Lord "just to remind the reader of the ambiguity," she says.

> Look first at the young king, a nation's pride, as bright and fortunate a soul as ever lived to the age of twenty-two; but when this picture was taken the young king had her back against a wall. She was filthy, she was trembling, and her face was blank and mad, for she had lost that minimal confidence in the world which is called sanity. Inside her head she repeated as she had been repeating for hours or years, over and over, "I will abdicate. I will abdicate. I will abdicate."[12]

The juxtaposition of the pronoun *she* with its antecedent "the young king" is brilliant. It jars the sensibilities of the native speaker of English to whom kings are male and *shes* are female and ne'r the twain shall be reconciled. Every man or woman who still thinks the choice of a pronoun is a trivial matter should read the story. Nor should you be surprised that when Winter's young king escapes to Earth she is called Mr Harge. As we all know, on the planet Earth the male is the norm. It is exactly right that in *The Left Hand of Darkness,* written from the point of view of a male Earthling, the androgynes are called *he*. Even when the Earthman confronts in his own consciousness that his friend is neither male nor female, he continues to refer to *him*.

Many educated readers with egalitarian leanings staunchly maintain that they can read through a passage with the generic *he* fully cognizant that both males and females are included. It is an acquired ability, but it is probably possible. What is not possible is for any native speaker of English to read through a passage using the "generic" *she* and think of anything but an exclusively female referent, unless, of course as Le Guin has shown, we are beguiled into doing so by exclusively male-designating nouns like *king* and *lord*. As an experiment in linguistic modification, it is far more likely that we will be able to de-masculinize nouns such as *doctor, welder, executive* and even *mail carrier* than that we will succeed in redefining the pronouns. To agree with the judgment *about syntax* that a singular generic pronoun is an absolute necessity and conclude, therefore, that in order to avoid sexism one can substitute the generic *she* is to invite a certain amount of ridicule and, more importantly, to slow down the acceptance of nonsexist language, if not to doom the struggle to failure early in the encounter.

The primary weapon of those who oppose feminist aspirations is ridicule. The power of ridicule should not be underestimated. The fear of being thought different can be seen most clearly in children. It is peer pressure to which they yield in their formative years and not to abstract moralizations. In order to have any chance of success in eliminating sexism from the language, you must choose alternatives which will not expose your attempts to automatic ridicule. You must, in essence, convince the reading public that it is possible to do what you and the government say is necessary.

The publishers' guidelines, as far as they go, are a step in the right direction since it is the publishers who ultimately decide what is standard written English and what is not. They are very much aware, however, of the difficulty involved from a stylistic point of view. McGraw-Hill provides a loop-hole, however, which endangers the whole enterprise:

> To avoid severe problems of repetition or inept wording, it may sometimes be best to use the generic *he* freely, but to add, in the preface and as often as necessary in the text, emphatic statements to the effect that the masculine pronouns are being used for succinctness and are intended to refer to both females and males.[13]

If invoked, this provision means that writers need not alter their comfortably sexist habits. The covert editorializing which is implicit in the generic *he* is declared by this provision to be at times unavoidable. And it certainly cannot be argued that formal and academic syntax of the sort which is commonly seen in textbooks and scholarly writing employs to a remarkable extent syntax which makes the singular pronoun *he* obligatory. The generic *he* is in fact one of the principal devices which writers customarily use to signal formality in writing. The pedantic mode, if we may call it that, is not by itself obligatory. It is often in fact quite removed from standard English. However customary pedantic syntax is, adopting the mode in the first place is not obligatory. If you set up a row of dominoes and bump the first one over, it is a law of nature that they will all fall; it is not a law of nature, however, that you must set up the row of dominoes in the first place or that you knock the first one over.

A lot of very bad writing is produced by writers in the business world straining after the elegance they feel is conveyed by this unnatural syntax. Writing plainly will not eliminate every instance of the generic *he* by any means. However, to suggest to anyone that they change

> As one grows older, he grows more conservative and more mellow

to the feminine form

> As one grows older, she grows more conservative and more mellow

when what they really mean is

> As you grow older (or as I grow older), you (or I) grow more conservative and more mellow

is no improvement. No native speaker of English who is male will do it unless he is writing exclusively about a woman or women or unless he is adopting a feminine persona in a piece of fiction.

Alternating *he* and *she*: works in unstereotyped examples

Whether or not the word *he* is ever actually understood by native speakers of English to include both males and females is still an open question for many people. Those who are writing on the subject are for the most part feminists, and they agree that *he* does exclude women. The research data summarized by Swift and Miller in *Words and Women* supports their contention.

Some people argue that, since English does not have a third person singular pronoun with common gender, the only fair thing to do is to alternate using *he* part of the time and *she* the rest. This is a solution which is being tried with increasing frequency. Dr. Lee Salk in his recent book, *Preparing for Parenthood,* remarked,

> An *author* interested in eliminating sexism from *his or her* work is immediately confronted with the masculine tradition of the English language. I personally reject the practice of using masculine pronouns to refer to human beings. Accordingly, I have freely alternated my references, sometimes using the female gender and sometimes using the masculine gender.[14]

Unfortunately, it will not work. *She* is not a common gender pronoun. It may be unfair, even immoral, but the pronoun *she* is in all circles–social, academic, and business–at all times unequivocally feminine. Two problems are likely to occur. The first is that the reader may mistake your *he* references to refer only to males and your *she* references to refer only to females. The second problem is that the writer may drift into stereotyping the *he* references with so-called masculine characteristics and the *she* references with what are perceived to be feminine characteristics. When this happens, you are right back where you started from. If the purpose in putting words down on paper is to increase communication, this unintended editorializing by either the writer or the reader will be an obvious impediment. You should not be misled by the apparent ease with which this solution seems to work into thinking that *she* will be absorbed into the language as an alternate generic form without some astonishing resistance.

The most militant promoters of the generic *she* recognize the unmistakable feminine connotation of *she* and, in fact, count on the unexpectedness of its use to shock the average reader into being reminded of the existence of women. It is an excellent argument because, of course, it works. The following paragraph by Sandra Scofield appeared in *Ms.* magazine in January 1977:

> When *a Montana rancher* wants information about *her* cattle or *her* land, *she* can call her county extension agent. But when *she* needs information about child abuse, menopause, abortion, and a host of other women's issues, *she* is likely to be the victim of *her* isolation. The messages of the Women's Movement have a lot of land to cover in Montana.[15]

In writing this paragraph the writer has cleverly made what is essentially a defect in formal written English work in her favor to carry by connotation far more information in a very few words than she ever could have accomplished by strictly adhering to the rule for the use of the generic *he*. Written out completely in language that is, according to traditional grammatical conventions, more denotative than connotative the passage would read something like this:

> When *a Montana rancher* wants information about *his* cattle or *his* land, *he* can call *his* county extension agent. Many Montana ranchers are women. The female ranchers of Montana have access to the same sort of information about land and cattle which is

> available to male ranchers. There is some information which may be necessary to women ranchers of Montana which is not of interest to male ranchers. This information is not as easily available, probably because it is not of interest to men. When *a woman* needs information about child abuse, menopause, abortion, and a host of other women's issues, *she* is likely to be the victim of *her* isolation. The messages of the Women's Movement have a lot of land to cover in Montana.

By using the pronoun *she* in the first sentence to refer to Montana ranchers, Scofield has cut through an enormous amount of verbiage which does nothing but detract from her central message which is that female ranchers have easy access to information which is traditionally sought by male ranchers but very limited access to information which is sought only by women. The passage works beautifully for the writer because she *uses* the fact that *she* is both connotatively and denotatively feminine. The subject of the first clause, "a Montana rancher," means "a typical rancher in Montana." Following the "a typical so-and-so" subject, if you are an educated reader and writer of English, you have a stereotyped image of a rancher and you expect the "generic" *he* to refer to *rancher*. Notice in the original paragraph that Scofield unnecessarily repeats *her* when she says, "When a Montana rancher wants information about *her* cattle or *her* land." She could just as easily have said, "*her* cattle or land," but instead she uses the opportunity to reinforce the unexpected *she* referent.

Using the supposedly "generic" *she,* Scofield does two things at once. She reminds you that not all ranchers are men, and she communicates to you about the relative ease of acquiring different types of information in Montana. The one thing she neither does nor attempts to do is to tell you that male ranchers of Montana are or ought to be as interested in child abuse, menopause, and abortion as female ranchers are. The paragraph as Scofield has written it operates to exclude male ranchers from the attention of the reader. The fact that it succeeds so well should, in addition, give pause to anyone still unconvinced that women are psychologically and semantically excluded by the consistent use of the generic *he.*

Now consider what would have happened if Scofield had used the logic that *he* and *she* are or ought to be interchangeable within a passage:

> When *a Montana rancher* wants information about *his* cattle or *his* land, *he* can call *his* county extension agent. But when *she* needs information about child abuse, menopause, abortion, and a host of other women's issues, *she* is likely to be the victim of *her* isolation. The messages of the Women's Movement have a lot of land to cover in Montana.

The preceding sentence is a made-up example, but it clearly illustrates the sort of stereotyping we are attempting to resist. It suggests that ranchers are male and women are menopausal. You may think this example is a bit extreme, so let's consider a real example, a first draft of a weekly report form to evaluate the progress of trainees. The supervisor is expected to mark that each trainee either does very well, is making satisfactory progress, or needs improvement. An explanation of each category is provided.

1. Attendance and promptness:

Does Very Well	Trainee is here every day and is on time. No excuses such as "overslept," "automobile breakdown," "ride did not come," etc. are acceptable.
Making Satisfactory Progress	This column will never be checked because either the *trainee* is here and on time every day or *he* is marked "Needs improvement."
Needs Improvement	Trainee is absent or tardy one or more times during the week.

This item can be considered fairly nonsexist. Since neither male nor female trainees can be marked "making satisfactory progress" so far as attendance and promptness are concerned, the use of the generic *he* is not particularly offensive. But now consider the second item. The writer is clearly conscious that there may be both male and female trainees; however, the trainee may well question whether there are different expectations for males and females in terms of "professional appearance."

2. Professional Appearance

Does Very Well	*Trainee* is consistent (every day) in terms of *his/her* appearance and personal hygiene habits. *She* presents the appearance of a professional elec-

	tronics technician consistent with the requirements of the profession.
Making Satisfactory Progress	*Trainee* is usually careful in terms of *his* appearance but occasionally is not up to the professional appearance desired.
Needs Improvement	*Trainee* frequently gives the appearance that *he* is not up to the level expected of technicians. Included are such items as unclean clothes, distracting articles of dress, etc., inconsistent with professional electronics technicians.

In exactly the same way that, unless told otherwise, you expect a doctor, welder, or editor to be male rather than female, this form suggests that trainees who are women are expected to be cleaner and better dressed than trainees who are men. In terms of promptness, the trainee is either "here and on time every day" or there are no excuses. In terms of appearance, however, *she* "does very well," while *he* is "making satisfactory progress" if only occasionally he is not presentable. The *his/her* under "does very well" suggests that males may also qualify for this designation, but that females must. The selective use of pronouns excludes women from the other two categories.

If a female trainee feels she is being discriminated against because in her experience there are different expectations for male and female trainees in terms of appearance, she might justifiably use this progress report sheet to substantiate her claim. It would be painfully ironical if the defense offered as an explanation for the form was that *he* and *she* were being alternated freely.

Pronoun alternation works fairly well when an author is describing discrete examples. Context and intention are the only criteria which can be applied for deciding whether a particular passage can be said to work. The McGraw-Hill guidelines provide a particularly effective example:

> I've often heard supervisors say, "She's not the right person for the job," or "He lacks the qualifications for success."

Notice, however, that what is really being alternated here is not pronouns but examples. The quotation marks around what supervisors have been heard to say puts the examples within a specific context. It is clear that sex is not being used as a criterion for deciding whether individuals should be promoted. If both examples had used the pronoun *he,* one could safely assume that not only were women not being promoted, they weren't even being considered for promotion. If both examples used the pronoun *she*, one could safely assume that sex was the criterion by which the candidates were being judged unacceptable for promotion or that this was a job held only by women. The pronouns themselves carry this information.

The example for alternating male and female examples and expressions offered by the NCTE guidelines is less effective:

> Let each student participate. Has she had a chance to talk? Could he feel left out?

In this example it is really the pronouns which are being alternated freely. Because the context is less specific, however, the passage is less clear. The desired effect of reminding the reader that both males and females are included in the class could have been achieved if the writer had focused on the examples themselves rather than on the pronouns:

> Let each student participate. Has Mary had a chance to talk? Could John feel left out?

The Macmillan guidelines do not offer alternating *he* and *she* as a viable solution. They say:

> The use of the masculine pronoun for hypothetical examples omits females, whether or not this is intended. The converse is true when feminine pronouns are used to describe activity assumed to be female.

Their examples include single sentences with clearly stereotyped examples:

TRY TO AVOID	SUGGESTED ALTERNATIVES
The prairie *farmer* was concerned about the price of *his* wheat.	Prairie *farmers* were concerned about the price of wheat.
The conscientious *housekeeper* dusts *her* furniture at least once a week.	The conscientious *housekeeper* dusts *the* furniture at least once a week.

Now consider the following passage from a recent book on human resource management:

> You will see improvement in the *individual's* skills, competency, commitment, and effort. *His* relationships with others will improve, *he* will begin to assume additional responsibilities, and will show a willingness to respond in a positive way to change. *He* will experience a sense of growth, progress, achievement. . . .[16]

Although this passage is sexist and offensive in its apparent assumption that either all human resources are male or else that only male resources are capable of growth and development, it is not as confusing as it would have been had the author chosen to alternate pronouns to avoid sexism:

> You will see improvement in the *individual's* skills, competency, commitment, and effort. *His* relationships with others will improve, *she* will begin to assume additional responsibilities, and will show a willingness to respond in a positive way to change. *He* will experience a sense of growth, progress, achievement. . . .

Two generalizations should be possible at this point. Alternating male and female examples can be both stylistically effective and nonsexist if the examples themselves are not stereotyped. However, alternating pronouns within a single passage can be confusing as well as ineffective.

The following selection was taken from a scholarly article discussing why students don't perceive errors within their own writing and contains a good example of a conscientious, nonsexist effort to alternate the pronouns *he* and *she.* This writer confines the alternations to separate paragraphs.

> With the first type of problem *a student* does not grasp a grammatical concept because of cognitive interference, and therefore can't see, understand, or correct errors in *his* writing. . . .
>
> With the second type of problem *a student* may not be able to apply a grammatical concept that *she* knows because of perceptual interference. For example, *she* may understand the use of inflection. . . .[17]

In this example the writer is in complete control of her syntax. The big danger is that she is not and cannot be in control of her readers' perceptions. Some readers might assume that only male students experience cognitive interference and only female students experience perceptual interference. A reader who has not been sensitized to what the author is doing will be jarred into wakefulness by the second paragraph. It is equivalent to encountering the passage by Le Guin in which she calls the young king *she*.

In English there is no such thing as a "generic" *she*. It is always possible to substitute a feminine example where the reader would customarily expect a masculine one, but it will rarely be possible to effectively substitute only the pronoun *she* for the generic *he*. Judge Marilyn Riddel in discussing her philosophy can say:

> All a *judge* can do is the very best *she* can with what is presented, and make a judgment as the law requires and the evidence warrants.[18]

because the referent is clearly herself. A male judge or someone discussing the problems and responsibilities of judges in general, if committed to the sentence as it stands, would have to pluralize *judges* or say, "All a *judge* can do is the very best *he or she* can. . . ."

Pacifying "paranoia":
(the parenthetical inclusion of women is insulting)

Those who wish to communicate to their audiences that they think being compelled to deal with sexism in language is an infringement on their freedom of expression usually signal this with the parenthetical remark. Some writers employ the parenthetica when they are adhering to the traditional grammatical and social conventions which say the male is the norm and the generic *he* is a necessary part of the language but when they are particularly aware of the fact (usually for a personal reason) that women are also included. After the words *man* or *he* used generically, they insert *or woman/or she* either enclosed in parentheses or set off by commas.

Whether intended as such or not, this technique is a veiled insult and assures the reader that the person who wrote it is fully aware of the transient nature of this latest fad. If used frequently, this method of "dealing with" sexism will tend to perpetuate the assumption that the human needs, aspirations, and interests of women are infantile and humorous. The attitude has some range, allowing the user to communicate everything from a patronizing pat on the head to a sneer, depending upon the context into which it is embedded.

The most innocuous display of this attitude appears when women are included as an afterthought. A report on Dr. Belle Bernstein's research on the role of the communicator in the corporate structure appeared in *Communication Notes* and said in part:

> She [Bernstein] sees the communicators' concerns focusing on four areas: the communicators' attitude toward themselves and their relationships with management, the rest of the organization, and their external public. The central picture that emerges from her discussion is of the high-level company *communicator* as the *man (or woman)* in a very uncomfortable middle—a person of high ideals who believes in the efficacy of communication to solve problems and to create an atmosphere of trust and cooperation within the company, but who is not trusted (and therefore not confided in) either by management or by the rank-and-file.[19]

In this paragraph the parentheses around *or woman* speak volumes. On a denotative level they say, "You'd expect a man to be a corporate communicator, of course, but surprisingly enough women hold this job also." The parenthetical nature of the inclusion of women is intrusive in the flow of the passage. Note in the last sentence of the quotation the effect of the second parenthetical expression: *and therefore not confided in*. It stands out; it calls attention to itself. However, where the second parenthetical expression is rhetorically appropriate, the first is not.

Any technique which calls attention to the fact that a human being is a woman will come out sounding patronizing. It is not necessary to pretend that she is a man to avoid this tone. Simply remove the parentheses:

> . . . The central picture that emerges from her discussion is of the high-level *communicator* as *the man or woman* in a very uncomfortable middle. . . .

Now, let's examine the passage from which this paragraph was extracted to see at what point the writer lost control of the message being conveyed. Remember that the writer has an attitude, the language used broadcasts an attitude, and the message is received by a reader with an attitude which will be either confirmed, challenged, or altered.

Let's assume that the writer here has either a positive or neutral attitude toward avoiding sexism and is merely adhering to the traditional rules governing the generic *he*. The difficulty is generated by the use of the word *man*. The writer is, no doubt, a native speaker of English who could have called an unknown writer, editor, communicator, welder, doctor, student, business executive, or tennis pro a *he*, but balked when it came to *man*. Being a native speaker of English, this writer knows that *men* are male but is also profoundly aware that not all communicators are men. From the writer's response to the word *man*, we would further guess that she is a female communicator.

The language itself interfered with the writer's perception of the message. He or she wanted to communicate, perhaps emphatically, that not all communicators are *men*. This is obvious since Dr. Bernstein, for one, is a woman and it's her report. Women have learned over the years that they are not supposed to take umbrage at the generic *he*, but the generic *he* coupled with the word *man* caused a profound reaction in this writer. Now you may say that is a lot of speculation about an individual to hang on a couple of little parentheses. But examine another passage from the same article:

> . . .The worst of it is that this dilemma is real, is daily, and has no easy solution. Management is right in thinking that *the communicator* might tell the worker–*his* professional integrity says that is exactly what *he* should do. The workers are right in seeing the communicator as a part of management–*his* company loyalty is second only to *his* professional loyalty.

By reverting to the generic *he* after this parenthetical exclamation that communicators are women as well as men, the effect of a message which may well have been intended to communicate, "I'm a woman and a corporate communicator and I'm damned sick of being called a man," is altered by grammatical convention to the parenthetical assertion that women are appropriately treated as parenthetical afterthoughts, and the message is then ready to be received by the reader.

The audience will consist of two basic types: those who are sensitive to the problems of avoiding sexism in communication and those who aren't. Those who aren't will be surprised by the parenthetical *or woman* and may notice the generic *he* where it otherwise would not have bothered them. For them the sex of the communicator has then become an issue which interferes with the primary message being communicated, that communicators are in an uncomfortable position between management and the rank-and-file. Those who are already sensitive to the problems of linguistic sexism will either wonder why a writer who is also aware of the problems persists in using the generic *he* or will agree with the unintentionally expressed notion that one has no choice but to toss women in parenthetically and proceed with the main business at hand.

A recent Nationwide insurance advertisement quite explicitly illustrates the patronizing attitude which can be conveyed through the parenthetical reference to the sex of the subject under discussion. The ad is entitled, "What your mother never told you about insurance." The connotation here is, of course, sexual, and *you* are presumed to be female. The ad says in brief that your mother didn't tell you about insurance because back in the olden days:

> Chances are, when your father's insurance agent dropped by, your mother was out in the kitchen fixing coffee and sandwiches. So she probably didn't know much to tell you.

Times have changed, the ad continues, and today's woman needs this information. However,

> Don't be upset with Dad, or Mom. They were only doing what was right back then.
>
> But do call a Nationwide agent. Ask *her*, or *him*, to fill you in on what you missed.[20]

The ad offends us first because of its sexual coyness. In our opinion, the ad trivializes profound social changes, attempts to capitalize on them, and calls attention to the sexual identity of its insurance agents in exactly the same way that putting *or woman* in parentheses after *man* does.

The coyness derives directly from putting the *or him* in as a parenthetical expression. You, the reader, as well as the ad writer know that insurance agents are more likely to be men than women. "Ask her, or him," has all the difficulties involved with trying to use the generic *she,* and it leads to a tone which strikes us as sneering. Clearly the ad was not intended to convey this message; however, the rhetorical choices made by the writer, compounded by the negative connotations which they convey to a person sensitive to sexism in communication, make the interpretation inevitable, although the company no doubt wants the insurance business of women.

Precisely the opposite tone was struck by a recent ad put out by the Martin Marietta Corporation. It showed three women and four men standing beside a fire truck with mountain scenery in the background and proclaimed:

> Meet the Crescent, Oregon Volunteer Fire Department: men, women, hard work, and pride."[21]

There is no cheesecake, no immature sexual overtones, and no patronizing suggestions. To destroy the ad, all they need to do is put *and women* in parentheses after *men,* instead of as a parallel element. This would express their shock and surprise at the fact that some of Crescent's firefighters are women and the tone of the ad would become, "See for yourself if you don't believe me: a bunch of chicks dressed up like firemen."

The Marietta Corporation, through this sort of matter-of-fact presentation, advertises itself as being progressive, egalitarian, and concerned about the environment, although they mention neither corporate profits, women's rights, or pollution control. The ad, of course, does not guarantee that any of these things are true. They may simply have a very smart ad agency while the other company does not. The insurance company may be deeply concerned that women with increased financial responsibilities are not adequately protected. If this is true, it is indeed unfortunate that an intelligent woman sensitive to sexism in communication must turn away from this insurance company's ad feeling either patronized or furious.

Recasting: a summary of your syntactic options

All of the acceptable alternatives to using the generic *he* likely to be adopted in organizational communications involve a certain amount of sentence revision. If you are able to eliminate sexism from your own writing while you are composing, rather than after your memo, report, or manuscript has been typed, you will suffer less anguish, and the final product will be smoother and more unified.

Basically the sentence revising strategies you can employ will involve either inserting references to women or recasting to eliminate the generic *he*. Those who write first and try to eliminate sexism afterwards invariably resort to inserting the feminine pronoun after the masculine in one of the following ways: *he or she, he/she, he (or she).*

If you use *he or she* judiciously, it is a workable technique for avoiding sexism. It works best in short passages where you don't have to switch cases. Try your hand at revising the following short passage right here in the book:

> Take your broker's suggestions seriously. He knows
>
> what the market has been doing, and he can predict
>
> what it will do in the future.

The pronoun *he* appears twice and refers back to *broker.* Since it is preferable not to repeat *he or she* in both places, one solution would be to add *or she* to the first *he* and to delete the second *he* altogether.

> Take your *broker's* suggestions seriously. *He or she* knows what the market has been doing and can predict what it will do in the future.

Compounding verbs in this manner will head off pronoun redundancy, which is the major pitfall with this solution. If you inserted *or she* after the first *he* without deleting the second *he*, you stumbled into the second pitfall: inconsistency.

Another solution which may sound better to you than the redundant use of *he or she* is to substitute the antecedent for the compound pronouns. For example:

> Take your *broker's* suggestions seriously. *A broker* knows what the market has been doing and can predict what it will do in the future.

Another thing you can do rather easily is to substitute a synonym for *broker.* For example:

> Take your *broker's* suggestions seriously. This *individual* knows what the market has been doing and can predict what it will do in the future.

If you choose to repeat the noun to which *he* refers or use a synonym, you still must watch out for inconsistency. After the word *and*, you must either delete *he* or say, "and *he or she* can predict. . . ."

With these considerations in mind, edit the following passage for sexist language.

> The communicator is concerned with integrity. He feels a sense of commitment and loyalty to his profession, and he wants management to appreciate that he is a communicator first, and then an organization man. The communicator is concerned with involvement. He wants to be involved, but he feels a sense of isolation in his job and expresses concern about this. He wants to de-isolate the communicator.

The solution to this passage which appeals to us most combines all of the techniques we have just discussed as well as the deletion of a repetitious sentence.

> The *communicator* is concerned with integrity, feels a sense of commitment and loyalty to the profession, and wants management to appreciate that *he or she* is a communicator first, and then a member of the organization.
>
> The communicator wants to be involved but feels a sense of isolation in the job and expresses concern about this. *He or she* wants to de-isolate the communicator.

The last sentence is the biggest problem in this passage. Technically *he or she* is acceptable because the compound pronouns are used only once in each paragraph. The sentence is difficult because of the disguised reflexive construction. It really means, "The communicator wants to de-isolate himself."

A single instance of *he or she* or even *him or her* will not be conspicuous, but most readers will find *himself or herself* obtrusive. It might be better to revise the last sentence to read:

> The communicator wants to de-isolate the job.
>
> or
>
> This person wants to de-isolate the job of the communicator.

In organizational communication your primary concern should appear to be the message you are sending and not your zeal for avoiding sexism. Under no circumstances should you add *or she* in parentheses because the parenthetical inclusion of women will always appear to be an afterthought and will distract the reader and detract from the effectiveness of your communication.

He/she resembles the *he or she* solution because you must also be concerned with consistency, redundancy, and the awkwardness of changing case, but it bears an uncomfortable resemblance to the parenthetical insertion of *or she*. The *he/she, him/her* solution is a graphic device clearly not meant to be read aloud. A version that some writers like is *s/he;* however, this breaks down when you must change to *him/her,* or *her/him*.

An example introduced earlier on page 25 contains *him/her* and illustrates the problems it can create for the careless. How would you revise the sentence to eliminate sexism and stylistic inconsistency?

> If television is substituted for a baby sitter–that is, the child is simply placed in front of the set while the parents ignore him/her–television becomes a major source of information about the reality of that particular home and/or society. In a sense, television becomes one of the "significant others," albeit an electronic one, from which the child gains information about his world.

To carry through with the slash solution, you either have to change *his world* to *his/her world* or to change *his world* to *the world*. We prefer the change to *the world* because this very short passage already contains two slashed constructions (*him/her* and *and/or*). The slashes become graphically overpowering and distract the reader's attention from your message. If you choose to use *he/she,* be consistent and always follow it with *him/her* and *his/her* rather than simply *him* or *his*.

Some people would rather visit the dentist than recast a sentence, but the perils involved in both experiences tend to be exaggerated. The most successful methods of avoiding sexism, because they are the least obtrusive, involve some recasting. The solution may be as simple as converting the possessive *his* to a neutral *a, an,* or *the* or deleting *his* altogether. This can often be done without disturbing another word in the sentence.

Eliminate the sexist use of *his* from the following sentences:

> The Director of Labor Force Studies will issue his report next month.
>
> Every manager must submit his revised budget to the Vice President of Finance within two weeks.
>
> A patient needs to see his family and friends while he is in the hospital.

In the first sentence, you should change *his* to either *a* or *the* depending upon context. In the second sentence, you must change *his* to *a* because it is implied that every department has its own budget. The third sentence is slightly more complex. First, you should delete *his* before family. Then to get rid of *he* you can simply delete *he is* or you can convert *while he is in the hospital* to *a hospitalized patient.*

> A patient needs to see family and friends while in the hospital.
>
> or
>
> A hospitalized patient needs to see family and friends.

Another construction which we should mention at this point is the use of the common gender *one* and its possessive *one's. One* is becoming obsolete, and as it does so, the forms which follow it are being replaced by the masculine pronouns.

> *One* always thinks the grass is greener on the other side of the fence until *he* gets there.

You can get rid of the sexist *he* and at the same time convert the sentence to a more conversational tone by recasting with *you.*

> *You* always think the grass is greener on the other side of the fence until *you* get there.

Try this editing strategy on the next sentence:

> One's brothers and sisters are a part of one's self.

You could have revised the sentence to read:

> *Your* brothers and sisters are a part of *your*self.

Or for an even more conversational tone, you can change *yourself* to *you.*

The "typical person" construction also lends itself to editing with *you.* Consider a passage which appeared earlier on page 22 and try to revise it.

> A motorist planning a trip must make a series of decisions. He must select a route of travel. He must decide upon a time of departure and arrival. He must determine how many hours he wishes to drive.

Given the direction to recast using *you,* it's quite possible that you may have left the first sentence alone, substituting *you* for every instance of *he,* although it is doubtful that you would have produced the construction writing from scratch because of the change from third person *motorist* to second person *you.* Any of the following alternatives would have been a better revision:

> If *you* are a *motorist* planning a car trip, *you* must make a series of decisions. *You* must select a route of travel. *You* must decide upon a time of departure and arrival. *You* must determine how many hours *you* wish to drive.

Or simply:

> If *you* are planning a car trip, *you* must make a series of decisions. *You* must select a route of travel, decide upon a time of departure and arrival, and determine how many hours *you* wish to drive.

Another way to change the passage would be to pluralize the singular noun *motorist* and then substitute *they* for each *he:*

> *Motorists* planning a car trip must make a series of decisions. *They* must select a route of travel. *They* must decide upon a time of departure and arrival. *They* must determine how many hours *they* wish to drive.

Pluralizing is a productive solution for eliminating sexism and has the added advantage of not suggesting that the typical anything (except father) is always male. Edit the following passage from page 26 for sexism and redundancy using the techniques we have discussed.

> The student will not know what is expected of him or her unless he or she has had an opportunity to work through the routine with his or her partner and then has repeated the procedure by himself or herself.

The big problem in this sentence is in preserving the one-to-one relationship between *the student* and a single partner. The sentence is from a set of instructions in which it is important that each student work through the routine with a single partner or either sex and then work through the routine alone. We have revised it in the following way:

> The *students* will not know what is expected of *them* unless each has had an opportunity to work through the routine with *a partner* and then to repeat the procedure *alone.*

You can also revise the sentence keeping *student* singular:

> The *student* will not know what is expected without an opportunity first to work through the routine with *a partner* and then to repeat the procedure *alone.*

Edit the following passage for sexism preserving the one-to-one relationship where it is essential. In some places the writers are generalizing about all salespeople and in another place, they are discussing the relationship between a single salesperson and a customer.

> Since satisfactory account relationships are an advantage to a marketer, the salesperson has two responsibilities: (1) to stress the long-term benefits of the account relationship to the customer, and (2) to help develop trust and credibility in himself and his company.
>
> There is a definite trade-off between "forcing" a customer to buy something and developing a long-term relationship with that customer. This trade-off can lead to a phenomenon called the "Pyrrhic sale," in which the sale is made at the expense of the account. In long-term relationships the customer is repeatedly in the position of being able to purchase the product. This circumstance requires the salesperson to manage the account carefully: if he (or she) forces a marginal sale, this often destroys credibility and the opportunity for future sales. But if the

> salesperson is willing to forego a sale that is not in the long-term interest of the account, he can build his relationship with that account.
>
> For example, the seller of apparel who is willing to tell a customer that some items in his line do not sell well at retail, in spite of their apparent appeal, helps his customer and himself over the long run. Or picture the response a buyer would give to the pump salesperson who says, "Yes, we offer the best pumps for your needs a, b, and c, but unfortunately, our pumps are not as good for application d as those offered by competitors x and y."[22] [Copyright 1976 President and Fellows of Harvard College]

In this passage the writers have used *salesperson* rather than the stereotyped *salesman*, and then halfway through the second paragraph they parenthetically throw in *or she,* so we know they are at least aware of the problem. Because of the one-to-one relationship in the third paragraph, however, a singular noun is more rhetorically effective than a plural one, and they have used the generic *he* throughout as a result. The solution to the first paragraph we like looks like this:

> Since satisfactory account relationships are an advantage to a marketer, *salespeople* have two responsibilities: (1) to stress the long-term benefits of the account relationship to the customer, and (2) to help develop trust and credibility in *themselves* and *their* company.

Putting the subject of this sentence, *salespeople,* in its plural form has the added advantage of indicating that a marketer is, no doubt, represented by more than one salesperson. We would revise the following paragraphs as follows:

> There is a definite trade-off between "forcing" a customer to buy something and developing a long-term relationship with that customer. This trade-off can lead to a phenomenon called the "Pyrrhic sale," in which the sale is made at the expense of the account. In long-term relationships the customer is repeatedly in the position of being able to purchase the product. This circumstance requires the *salespeople* to manage *such accounts* carefully: if *they* force a marginal sale, this often destroys credibility and the opportunity for future sales. But if *they* are willing to forego a sale that is not in the long-term interest of *an account, they* can build the relationship with that account.
>
> For example, the *seller* of apparel who is willing to tell a customer that some items in *a line* do not sell well at retail, in spite of their apparent appeal, helps the customer and *the seller* in the long run. Or picture the response a buyer would give to the pump salesperson who says, "Yes, we offer the best pumps for your needs a, b, and c, but unfortunately, our pumps are not as good for application d as those offered by competitors x and y."

Sometimes more extensive revision of a sentence is necessary. Your commitment to the order of the words as they stand will be the strongest deterrent to inconspicuously avoiding sexist language.

Often a sentence unnecessarily repeats the subject through the use of the generic *he*. Edit the following sentences:

> These three incidents all show how easily with modern techniques the biologist can stumble, almost before he has realized it, into making research organisms of potentially grave hazard.

> If a student proficiencies out of a module but consistently continues to produce the error in his writing, this is adequate indication that he needs more work.

> When an unpublished author sees no way of getting his book accepted by a commercial publisher, he can go to a vanity press.

It is important to remember while working through these exercises that practice with many different sentence structures will eventually make the problem much simpler to deal with. The first sentence should be fairly easy. The solution which disturbs the sentence least appears to be:

> These three incidents all show how easily with modern techniques the *biologist* can stumble, almost *before realizing it,* into making research organisms of potentially grave hazard.

This was the only sentence in an article which ran close to a thousand words with sexist overtones, and the assertion that biologists must be male is purely gratuitous.

The second sentence involves more rearrangement. If you realize as you write *a student* that you mean to say *the typical student,* you can predict an encounter with the generic *he* and avoid it before it arises; however, you can keep the subject, *a student,* singular only if you are willing to recast:

> If *a student* proficiencies out of a module, consistent production of the error in writing is adequate indication that *more work is needed.*

In addition to eliminating sexism, the revision saves four words even though it employs the passive voice in the final clause. You have, no doubt, been taught to avoid passive constructions. They have been called "less direct, less bold, and less concise" than sentences written in the active voice. The advice to avoid them is derived from the larger injunction to make "every word tell," but to adhere to the active voice at the risk of invoking the generic *he,* you may tell more than you intend.

The third example contains another instance of the "typical person" syndrome, in this case the typical unpublished author. The solution here involves a construction you are likely to use often:

> An unpublished *author* who sees no way of getting a book accepted by a commercial publisher can go to a vanity press.

Clearly more revision is necessary in order to maintain a singular subject. Unless a one-to-one relationship between the typical author and publisher is important to the passage in which it appears, you may prefer to simply pluralize *author.*

> Unpublished authors who see no way of getting *their* books accepted by a commercial publisher can go to a vanity press.

Once you become convinced that using the generic *he* carries with it a connotation you cannot endorse, you will become far more adept at eliminating it from your own writing. Unless you mean to imply that women exist in the business world as atypical accidents, you do all women, the organization you work for, and yourself a disservice by persisting in the use of an archaic, demeaning, and inaccurate convention.

3 Forms of Address

Sex and Salutation

"I'd like to introduce you to John Smith.
He isn't married."

If you are uncomfortable not knowing the marital status of women, you might ask yourself why you are *not* uncomfortable not knowing the marital status of men. You would, in fact, be quite surprised if a man were introduced to you for the first time with this information attached. Such an introduction would ordinarily be taken as a joke, probably at John's expense. Yet it is perfectly normal to introduce a businesswoman as *Miss* or *Mrs.* However, unless you consider the marital availability of female employees an appropriate piece of information to convey in business communications, it should not be there. If you do believe that marital status is an appropriate piece of information to be conveyed in business communications and if your legal department does not dissuade you, you certainly wouldn't want to discriminate against men by not providing data on their marital status. Ambrose Bierce in *The Devil's Dictionary* suggested that if we must have marital titles for women, we ought to have them for men too. He suggested *Mush,* which would be abbreviated *Mh.,* for unmarried men. Presumably *Mr.* would be restricted to married men.

Amusing as such a practice might be, we do not recommend it. It is as inappropriate to include a man's marital status in every day business communications as it is to include a woman's. Besides even if a woman is married, she may not be using her husband's last name, and you will call her *Mrs. Mary Daley* when in fact her husband's last name is Smith. Many women in business, especially young women, feel that giving up their own names is like giving up a part of their personal identity, legal standing, and social autonomy. Happily married and accomplished women of all ages can love their husbands and at the same time resent the implication in the title *Mrs. John Smith* that they are possessions of or mere adjuncts to a husband. When the pressure is on at work, Mary is as much on the spot as her coworkers Joe and Dave. At work her accomplishments are her own; John is as detached from them as are the spouses of Joe and Dave.

The history of Mrs.: it signalled marital status only recently

Although the courtesy title *Mrs.* has been around since at least 1582 according to the OED, it is only fairly recently that it has been used to signal marital status. Originally *Mrs., Mis.,* and *Miss.* were all abbreviations for *Mistress* and were originally pronounced just like *mistress,* not like *Mi-sis* or *mi-siz.* All three were equivalent to the masculine courtesy title *master* and were used before the names of young and old, married and unmarried females when they had no superior title. In this earliest period someone might have written of "Mrs. Mary, who is seven years old" and not raised an eyebrow because all the writer intended to convey with *Mrs.* was that Mary came from a respectable family. However, some time in the 17th century *mistress* and its abbreviations, like many terms applied to women, acquired derogatory meanings like "concubine" and even "prostitute." Forms attached to proper names as titles of respect escaped this connotation however, but in the process they acquired a pronunciation different from that of *mistress.* In this period the word *mistress* split into two abbreviations used to signal age: *Mrs.* for all adult women married or not and *Miss.* for all female children.

It was not until the beginning of the nineteenth century that *Mrs.* signalled marital status, not age. You'll recall that Mrs. Bridges, the cook on the television program "Upstairs, Downstairs," had never been married. *Mrs.* was simply a title of respect affixed to her name as a sign of her status and age.

At one time marriage and a career were so generally considered to be mutually exclusive that the belief became a self-fulfilling prophecy. An employer assumed that a young working woman was only a temporary employee. She was considered a poor risk for expensive training programs, denied promotion because she lacked formal training, and relegated to the most boring, repetitious, and low-paid work. With so little incentive to stay, it is not surprising that most women did leave the labor force when they married.

The marital status of female employees should be only as relevant to an organization as is the marital status of its male employees. A company anxious to eliminate discriminatory employment practices should as a matter of course discontinue using marital titles in organizational communications. This is a very touchy subject for many older women, but fortunately the older women most likely to be offended by the absence of their marital title are probably not in the work force. Let's consider your options.

Omit all marital titles: probably the best idea

If you are already omitting the courtesy title *Mr.* for men, the most straightforward thing to do is to omit all titles for women too. It is already standard practice for the *Tom O'Hara* you write about in the first paragraph to become *O'Hara* thereafter; *Carol Josephs* should be referred to as *Josephs* in all subsequent references. Be consistent: make particularly sure you don't use men's last names and women's first names, although of course you might wish to firstname both men and women after the first paragraph in informal communications within a small organization. If you think about it you'll realize that a person's first name is often used to define power relationships. Women, children, servants, and others considered inferior are traditionally firstnamed, and they of course are expected to respond using last names.

Use *Ms.* or professional title: be consistent

If a woman has a professional title and if you are writing about her in that context, it goes without saying that you should use her professional title. If she is Senator, Doctor, Professor, or Judge Smith, say so, just like you would with a man.

If you do use the courtesy title *Mr.* for men, you can always use *Ms.* for women. The rationale behind this title was explained in the first issue of *Ms.* magazine which appeared in the spring of 1972:

> *Ms.* is being adopted as the standard form of address by women who want to be recognized as individuals, rather than being identified by their relationship with a man.

Attitudes toward the term *Ms.* are a very revealing index to a person's willingness to change and accept change. An organization which five years after its introduction refuses to allow the innocuous designation *Ms.* is perpetuating the sexist notion that the marital status of female employees is a necessary piece of public information in a way that a male employee's marital status is not. It would be very foolish, however, to restrict your use of *Ms.* to your unmarried female employees and to continue referring to all married women in the organization as *Mrs.* This is tantamount to the insulting and hypocritical practice of referring to a male committee head as *chairman* and to a female (or minority member) committee head as *chairperson.*

If the person you are writing about specifically requests that you handle her marital status in a particular way, we believe you should bow to her wishes, whatever your standard policy. The novelist Jean Stafford, for example, has said that she wants to be referred to as *Miss Stafford* if the subject is her writing or her business and as *Mrs. Liebling* if inquiries are being made about her late husband. We find it annoying and pretentious that the New York *Times* refuses to honor Billie Jean King's request that she be called *Ms. King* and instead refers to her as *Mrs. King,* although we do prefer the *Times's* practice of referring to Patricia Hearst as *Miss Hearst* instead of *Patty*.

In the business world, however, a woman should ***never*** be known by her husband's name (i.e., *Mrs. John Smith*). If she insists upon the inclusion of the marital status marker, she should be referred to as *Mrs. Clara Smith*. Consider how amused you would be if the spouse of Clara Smith were referred to as *Mr. Clara Smith*.

Business letter salutations: don't despair

Ironically it is a very brief item, the salutation of a letter, where avoiding sexism can be most vexing. There simply is no widely accepted polite equivalent for *Dear Sir* or *Gentlemen* because of the unfortunate connotation of *Madam*. You can attack this problem most directly by considering the nature of your communication, the style which is most appropriate to your purpose, and your own intentions.

Beginning a letter to an individual: it's best to use a name

In general, letters to individuals are no problem because you usually write to persons whose name and sex you know. If you are answering a letter from a person whose first name does not clearly signal sex or a letter from a person who used initials instead of a first name in the close, the obvious thing to do is to address the person in the same way (i.e., *Dear Hilary Smith* or *Dear H. L. Smith*). This is the sane thing to do. We know of a couple of businesswomen who are regularly the recipients of *Dear Mr.* - - - - - - - letters who welcome situations like this so they can turn the tables and write *Dear Ms. Smith* to all persons of unknown sex. It is unlikely that a man would choose to do this, however, and we do not recommend this as a standard practice.

A second viable option for handling the salutations of letters to individuals whose last names you know but whose sex you don't know is to use other courtesy titles they might possess like *Doctor* or *Professor* (i.e., *Dear Doctor Smith* or *Dear Professor Smith).*

If you are not responding to a letter and so lack even the last name of the individual to whom you are writing, you can write *Dear Editor* or *Dear Director of Labor Force Studies*. If at all possible, however, you should get the name of the individual who holds the position.

Beginning a letter to an organization: eschew false fondness

Did *Dear Director of Labor Force Studies* make you a little jumpy? If it did, it's probably because of the discrepancy between the connotations of affection and esteem which attach to *Dear* and the cold impersonality which attaches to the title *Director of Labor Force Studies.* Is the Director really dear to you? Certainly not, if you don't know the individual's name. In cases like these we recommend that you switch tone altogether and either move to a modified memo style (i.e., *Attention: Director of Labor Force Studies* or *Attention: Order Department*) or omit the salutation entirely, beginning your letter right after the address of the organization to which you are writing. These are your most businesslike options.

Those who wish to inject an unbusinesslike tone into organizational communications and those who wish to make a point of *not* writing *Dear Sir* have adopted the salutations *Dear Gentleperson* and *Dear Gentlepeople.* This is not a strategy we recommend for regular usage because it strikes us as somewhat precious, but if you have been provoked by a letter which got your sex wrong or by an obviously computer-generated letter, you may wish to retaliate with *Gentleperson.* In our experience such a salutation leads inevitably to a somewhat whimsical tone; however, if you and the others follow the salutations *Gentlepeople* and *Gentleperson* with messages written in an ordinary businesslike tone, these salutations may very well catch on since they fill a definite need. The salutation *Ladies and Gentlemen* will almost surely not catch on because it is an expression which is restricted almost entirely to speechmaking.

Actually this is another instance where we'll have to fumble around for a while until the language decides what it's going to do. Textbooks currently being written on business communication will greatly influence which of the salutation options we've described is most widely used. Unfortunately many authors and publishers of books on organizational communication are sitting on the fence at the very time the probability of a woman being addressed as *Dear Sir* mounts, but this is no excuse for you to continue using the sexist salutation. Although many of the publishers who will put these texts on the market have issued guidelines for avoiding sexism, none of the guidelines we've seen addresses the problem of beginning a letter to a person of unknown sex. Business communication must continue despite the fact that no single solution has been offered by the publishers. Interestingly enough, the choices which you make about salutation forms will influence the people you write to, and ultimately what the business community does will influence what the publishing companies decide is acceptable.

4 Sex Role Stereotyping

Words and Slurs

A San Francisco radio station in the recent past wrote and ran a spot announcement for a drug dependency unit looking for volunteer doctors and therapists. The announcement concluded, "If you're a chick, they need typists." Although it is inconceivable that they could have included in their solicitation for volunteers a welcome to any black person who could push a broom, when they received calls protesting the blatant sex role stereotyping they revised the announcement to "If you're a chick and can type, they need typists."

It is clear that whoever wrote this announcement made a number of stereotyped assumptions. First, the writer (we assume it was *he*) thought that women are flattered to be called *chicks* since it seems unlikely that he would knowingly insult a person he wanted to do some free typing. This is not a safe assumption. Second, the writer either assumed that therapists (more than 75% of whom are women according to the Bureau of Labor Statistics) and doctors were all men or he decided that professional women in these categories would not respond to being called *chicks*. The latter is certainly a safer assumption.

Racial slurs which reach the public either by broadcast over the air or in print are grounds for termination at all levels of employment. The embarrassment of the Ford administration by a racist joke attributed to the Secretary of Agriculture is a prominent example. And yet within a few weeks of that disgraceful incident Johnny Carson had the audacious bad taste to call Barbara Walters a "news lady of the evening," over national television without, to our knowledge at this writing, being sued for defamation of character. And Jim Wright (D-Texas), the newly elected Majority Leader in the House of Representatives, when asked to state a broad rule for avoiding Congressional sex scandals, is quoted as proposing: "The Wright broad rule is that broads ought to be able to type."[23] The implications of this remark are clear. The word *broad* has sexual connotations which suggest that women are appropriately categorized as sex objects, and the suggestion that "broads should be able to type" indicates that these sex objects are appropriately relegated to low status jobs such as typing.

There is, after all, nothing intrinsically demeaning about being a secretary. Secretaries are the people who hold offices together; they get things done; they must be analytical, meticulous, personable, and energetic. The only thing wrong on a professional level with being a secretary is that they are not paid what they are worth to any organization. To add insult to this financial injury by calling them *babes, dolls, girls,* or *broads* is at its most innocuous level a form of depersonalization. These infantile and sexual categorizations are totally inappropriate in a public organization such as a business or corporation and should be shunned. It goes without saying that women in government deserve the same respect.

Women should no more be jokingly referred to as *chicks* and *broads* by DJ's and members of Congress than adult black males should be called *boys.* As women increasingly protest this sort of gratuitous insult, sexist slurs will become as socially, economically, and politically inexpedient as racist slurs are now.

Basically sexist stereotyping comes in four varieties. The first consists of labels which confine women to sexual or infantile roles. Words like *broad* or *babe* are prominent examples. Even if you know individual women who do not object to such terms, it is no longer safe to assume that such familiarity will be tolerated, much less welcomed, by the general female population.

A second kind of linguistic stereotyping involves bypassing the individuality of women and describing them as virtuous when they keep in the place men have assigned to them. They become *the better half, "the" wife,* or *the fair sex.*

A third form of sexist description involves terms which signal the feminine gender on supposedly common gender nouns – *lady lawyer* and *authoress* are good examples.

A fourth form of stereotyping excludes women entirely. This usually involves the ending *-man* on a job title. The Manpower Administration has revised its occupational titles to delete age and sex referent language to come into compliance with the Civil Rights Act of 1964 and with the Age Discrimination in Employment Act of 1967.[24] You can obtain a copy of these revisions from the Department of Labor. Here is a list in alphabetical order of some of the more common or egregious varieties of sexist vocabulary items and our recommended alternatives.

Words and expressions to avoid

Avoid	**Use**
authoress	author
the best man for the job	the best qualified candidate for the job, the best person for the job, or the best man or woman for the job
the better half	wife
brotherhood (and fellowship and fraternity)	friendship, unity, kinship, companionship, community, oneness, or peace
businessman	business executive, business leader, entrepreneur, manager, operator of a small business, merchant, or industrialist

Words and expressions to avoid

Avoid	Use
camera girl	photographer
cameraman	camera operator
career girl	professional, professional woman, or name the woman's profession (i.e., lawyer)
chairman	leader or moderator (of a meeting), chair, coordinator, head (of a committee), presiding officer (of a company), or chairperson
cleaning woman or cleaning lady	house or office cleaner
co-ed	student
the common man	the average person or ordinary people
Congressman	Member of Congress or Congressional Representative
craftsman	skilled worker or name the occupation (i.e., electrician)
draftsman	drafter
the fair sex	women
fireman	firefighter

Words and expressions to avoid

Avoid	Use
foreman	supervisor
gal, girl	woman
gal Friday	assistant
girl—as in "I'll have my *girl* do it."	secretary
housewife	homemaker, customer, shopper, or consumer
insurance man	insurance agent
ladies—when men are called *men*, not *gentlemen*	women
lady—as a modifier as in *lady lawyer*	lawyer (or whatever the woman's occupation)
libber	feminist
the little woman	wife
longshoreman	longshore worker
mailboy	mail clerk, mail messenger
mailman	mail carrier, letter carrier, or postal worker
man—used generically	person or human being

Words and expressions to avoid

Avoid	Use
-man—used as an agent ending as in *pipeman*	-er as an agent ending; or describe just which duties or actions are being performed (i.e., pipe adjuster, pipe agent, pipe attendant, pipe broker, pipe cleaner, pipe controller, pipe inspector, pipe installer, pipe maker, pipe patcher, pipe setter, pipe tender, pipe tester, and most general of all, pipe worker
manned	staffed
man and wife	husband and wife, man and woman, or the couple
manhood	adulthood or maturity
mankind	humanity, human beings, or people
man-made	synthetic, machine-made, or manufactured
manpower	labor force, work force, workers, human energy, or human power
a man-sized job	a big or enormous job
middleman	go-between, liaison, broker, or intermediary
milkman	milk route driver
the old lady	wife

Words and expressions to avoid

Avoid	Use
old wives' tales	superstition or superstitious beliefs
poetess	poet
policeman	police officer
right-hand man	assistant or key person
salesman	sales clerk, sales representative, sales agent, sales person (sales people), or sales force
spokesman	speaker or spokesperson
statesman	leader, diplomat, public figure, or public servant
stewardess	cabin attendant or flight attendant

Words and expressions to avoid

Avoid	**Use**
sweet young thing	young woman or girl
usherette	usher
watchman	guard
the weaker sex	women (or men, depending on your perspective)
"the wife"	wife or my wife
woman's work	This is a meaningless concept; delete altogether.
workmen's compensation	worker's compensation
workman	worker
workmanlike	competent or professional

5 Writing about Women

Some Insulting Formulas You Should Avoid

> "I'm Barbara Anne Maquire—your Allied driver—and I will be handling your move." These words generally come as a surprise to a customer expecting a van foreman. . . . (*The Allied Shield*, July/August 1976)

There are several interlocking purposes behind writing about an employee in an organizational publication. One purpose is to acquaint the rest of an organization with the individual and through the person increase company awareness of the interdependent nature of all the jobs performed at every level. Another effect of singling out an individual is to publicly honor the person interviewed and in a small way to reward the hard work and skill of a valuable member of the organization. The pride and gratitude of the individual you focus on can have a halo effect on everyone around, and the pay-off comes in improved company relations.

Although it may be just another story to you, to the employee it may be a unique experience. What you write about each employee will follow the individual through the organization. Now is not the time to resort to sexist formulas for describing a woman. Meaningless cliches, which are all too common, detract from the person's individuality, trivialize the person's accomplishments, and may inadvertently patronize the person written about. Let's examine some of the sexist presumptions illustrated by frequently occurring descriptions of women. These sexist expressions are used so regularly that they have become formulas.

Do not comment on sexual desirability of businesswomen

Writers seem to feel obliged to comment on the physical (which is to say sexual) desirability of every woman they write about. Calling all women *pert* or *attractive* has become so automatic as to be meaningless. The New York *Times* even referred to a judicial candidate as having "a beauty queen figure," though the physical condition of the male candidates being considered was not mentioned. This kind of physical description also occurs in company publications with tiresome regularity and is just as inappropriate.

Let's examine in detail one very instructive article in which a company communicator is inadvertently undermining a company's inclusion of a serious and ambitious woman in a previously all-male meeting.

> A *pretty lady* working in the Dye House at the Blanket Finishing Mill?
>
> That's right. Her name is Melba Denise Prince. She's a rising senior at N.C. State University and one

> of a number of college students who are participating in Fieldcrest's Summer Intern Program this year.
>
> Majoring in textile chemistry, the *petite* student is interested in the dyeing and finishing processes of the textile industry. After graduation next year, she hopes to find a management job with a textile company and hopes also to work in a Dye House. . . .
>
> It's easy to understand why the Blanket Finishing Dye House employees (*all male*) find Denise a welcome addition to their department. "She's not only *very pretty* and *very pleasant, but* she's a hard worker, too," they say. (The *Mill Whistle,* July 19, 1976)

The picture of Melba Denise Prince which accompanied the story is sufficient testimony to her youth and attractiveness. Introducing the story with a question unmistakably reinforces the stereotyped counter-expectation that a woman who is sexually attractive would not choose this job. Why she's pretty enough to "catch" a man. The writer's stereotyped assumptions of what is proper for a young attractive woman are underlined throughout the article by a series of rhetorical contrasts. The question form is the first such contrast. The third paragraph contains another contrast with what the writer perceives to be a traditionally masculine interest in the chemistry with the intern's femininity, which is expressed through the word *petite. Petite* is a loaded word which should be avoided. On a denotative level *petite* means small or minor in significance; on a connotative level it means feminine. No one would refer to a man as *petite, cute, short, attractive,* or even *handsome* in a serious article because such designations would detract from the purpose of the article, to describe his accomplishments. We strongly recommend testing any descriptive phrases you are tempted to apply to a woman by asking yourself whether you would use them or ones like them to describe a man.

Later in the article the writer uses sexual innuendo in describing the young intern's relationship with the other employees. The parenthetical insertion, *all male,* contrasted with *it's easy to understand* implies that she is accepted not for her professional skills but for her physical charms. It forcibly raises the question of whether a professionally accomplished but less attractive woman would be as quickly accepted in this environment.

The statement imputed to her co-workers that she is not only friendly and attractive *but* a hard worker makes it sound as if these qualities were mutually exclusive. This is one of the most destructive myths in our culture. It operates to keep women "in their place."

In our society women have been regarded as being of two kinds. There is the virtuous wife and mother, and there is the prostitute. In writing about women, authors have a deplorable tendency to relegate women by description or implication to one role or the other with varying degrees of subtlety.

The virtuous woman is easily identified by the parenthetical insertion of the number of her offspring immediately following her name. The formula typically runs like this:

> Carol Bradley, *mother of four,* was elected Mayor by a narrow margin. . . .

Women whether they have been elected to Congress, appointed Ambassador, or given the Pulitzer Prize are routinely described in this manner, and the formula has been picked up by company writers. Even when varied slightly, the formula is easy to spot:

> For Maude Campbell, *a great-grandmother* who keeps her exact age a secret, it was a reliving of 22 June 1926, when she was a *female daredevil* who winged her way into aviation history by becoming the first *woman passenger* on a commercial airline. (McDonnell Douglas *Spirit,* July 1976)

Ask yourself whether you would write this:

> John Jones, a great-grandfather, ...

This is not to deny that employees have personal lives which may be of interest to readers. However, putting the number of children immediately after the first use of the person's name has the effect of defining the person in terms of his or her children. And, of course, in a company publication the person should be defined in professional terms. In doing a brief sketch of a worker, putting the family in a separate paragraph has two decidedly positive consequences. First it does not distract the reader from the person's professional capacity, and second it puts the family itself in a more important light.

In a company publication, discussion of the family should follow discussion of the job. An article from *Cross Section* on Pauline Chlystek's retirement dinner balanced its treatment of her job as an archivist with her personal life reasonably well. It began with a quotation from her husband:

> "Commonwealth had Paulie for 21 years. Now I get her for the rest!"
>
> Those were Frank Chlystek's words as he spoke of his wife Pauline's career at her retirement party on May 21.
>
> Friends and associates, 125 strong, helped Pauline mark her retirement with a dinner at Point East in Jackson. A skit, speeches and gifts highlighted the occasion.
>
> Pauline spent her career handling retrievals of tracings for engineers and clients in Jackson's Records Center. . . . (Gilbert Commonwealth *Cross Section,* July 1976)

Eleven paragraphs later we find out about her children and grandchildren.

Now consider the next headline and lead sentence for a news release from the Georgia Pacific Corporation:

> *MOTHER OF FIVE IS LUMBER MILL MECHANIC, WELDER, UNION CHIEF*
>
> Can a Kentucky *mother of five children* find happiness as a lumber mill mechanic and union president 'way Down East in Maine?
>
> Norma Smith did. . . .(Georgia-Pacific Corporation *News Feature Facts,* June 1976)

Norma Smith's accomplishments are trivialized by the soap opera parody employed by the writer, although it is conceded later in the story that Smith "takes a no-nonsense approach to the job of representing some 75 men and 15 women workers at the plant." If our choice of the word *conceded* seems harsh to you, remember that all a reader has to go on is what you say. Stereotyped allusions inevitably call up stereotyped images.

The catchy lead-in to too many articles about women depends on sexual stereotyping which, intentionally or not, it reinforces. The soap opera refrain at least established subliminally that Smith was a respectable woman. The next example puts the subject, a female coach of a high-school boys' golf team, in the opposite light. The lead-in maintains:

> Good coaches come in an assortment of *sizes, shapes,* and *hairdos.* (*Chicago Daily News,* September, 1976)

After some discussion of the young woman's undeniable qualifications to coach golf, the writer asks:

> What's a nice girl like Lisa doing in coaching?

This, as most readers surely know, is a parody of the stereotyped question men supposedly ask prostitutes, "What's a nice girl like you doing in a place like this?" Like the soap opera refrain, this is an easily identifiable allusion. The sexual overtones keep the reader's interest at the expense of the person being written about.

The communicators who rely on this sort of cheap shot hurt the person written about, their company, and their own professional reputations. You should always remember that the purpose of these articles is to promote the company's interests by honoring the individuals written about. The parenthetical aside adds color to an article and it should be used to do so. But be aware that in the parenthetical aside you can speak volumes in attitude and undo a well-done article.

Select detail carefully and honestly

Attitudes are clearly expressed through non-essential descriptive prose. In the following article about the increasing number of women who own and manage farms, the writers use stereotyped feminine markers to contrast society's expectations and actual women farmers. The important thing to notice in these examples is the scrupulous avoidance of the sexual put-down:

> Like many working women, Lucille Crawford rises before dawn, eats a hearty breakfast, teases her hair and clips on a pair of gold earrings. Then the 54-year-old widow dons a green-and-yellow cap, climbs into a bronze pickup truck and sets out for a sixteen-hour day tending her 200-acre farm in Ashland, Ill. . .

And

> Mary Holz-Clause represents the new breed of women farmers. "When I have to put down my occupation, I put down 'farmer' and I'm proud of it," she says. Mary's husband, Reginald Clause, is now teaching her how to weld. Then, she says, maybe she'll learn how to sew. (*Newsweek,* November 9, 1976)

We consider the second example more effective than the first because the woman speaks for herself. She herself recognizes the difference between society's expectations and her own interests. The first example depends on the writer's observations. As a formula, such an introduction is fraudulent if the detail is tacked on by the writer. The descriptive detail should be the most personal and the least stereotyping information you can convey about your subject.

Just as when you write about men, the details you select should be functional and not merely formulaic tags like *pert, attractive,* and *mother of four.* In the following example a piece of personal information, age, provided an important focal point:

> At age 55, Mary Gardiner Jones took her first job in industry last year. It was a good start: $55,000 a year as vice-president of Western Union Telegraph Co., the principal subsidiary of Western Union Corp. It is a slot the company brass had set aside specifically for a woman, in an area in which women executives are doing especially well–consumer affairs.
>
> Does this sex stereotyping bother her? "Hell, no–it gives me a foot in the door," she says. "You know, I've been barred for so long, the fact that I'm now coming into my own–and perhaps with a slight advantage–is a rather pleasant experience for me." (*Business Week,* August 16, 1976)

Discuss changing attitudes

The subject of past discrimination is an uncomfortable one for many companies and individuals. The company communicator is an advocate for both the company and individual employees. Neither will be served, however, by playing one against the other in the issue of past discrimination. Nonetheless, women's attitudes towards their roles in society and in the organization cannot be neglected. The writer should strike a matter-of-fact tone, concentrating on current progress rather than past discrimination. A recent issue of *The Digest,* a Xerox Company publication, was devoted to the changing roles of women and handled the problem well. Claire Smith, an employee who moved from the position of file clerk to Manager of equipment and supplies for Materials Management, addressed the problems confronted by a woman in a formerly male position:

> She's straightforward and minces no words in describing her views. "Climbing the managerial ladder is not an overnight feat–it comes with years of experience, hard work and a lot of guts," she says. "Being in the right place at the right time may be helpful initially, but to retain your position and advance you have to be able to pull your own weight."
>
> Smith believes women have to be smarter and more assertive than their male counterparts just to be taken seriously. She also believes that dedication, hard work, being able to cope with pressure and your own fears of failure are absolute requirements for women in management. (Xerox *Digest,* August 27, 1976)

One of the most effective techniques in this special issue of *The Digest* was the exploration of male employees' attitudes toward the changing roles of women in Xerox.

> Everette Taylor is a work order coordinator in the Fabrication/Assembly plant. He believes that working at Xerox has contributed a great deal in changing his attitudes towards working women. "At first I wondered why some women were taking away men's jobs until I began to question–just what makes me think that a job should belong to a man specifically? I realized that if women are qualified, why not? I personally don't feel threatened by the added competition. It just makes me work harder," he says.
>
> Like many other men nowadays, Taylor often helps out at home. They are awaiting the arrival of

> their second child now, but he says that when his wife was working he often started dinner and has never been afraid to push the vacuum cleaner around. (Xerox *Digest*, August 17, 1976)

Letting employees speak for themselves is a good idea, but the communicator has a responsibility to the company and the individual interviewed and must use editorial judgment to promote the long-term interests of both.

> . . .A confirmed "non-women's libber," Evelyn does not wish "to exchange her 'superior' rights for lesser 'equal' ones." (Mutual Trust Life Insurance Company *Record,* July 1976)

In our judgment, sexist remarks by individuals of either sex are as offensive as racist ones. Although we recognize that there are people who still find them amusing, including such bigotry in a company publication harms the organization and the person quoted by offending all of those who believe the aspirations of women are as legitimate as those of men.

Examine your own assumptions

One of the things which makes avoiding sexism so difficult for some writers is that they have not examined their own assumptions carefully enough. These stereotyped assumptions reveal themselves in dependent clauses and parenthetical insertions. For example, a writer discussing the career of Nathalie Hoca, general manager of Cartier, wrote:

> . . .but she was only 22 when her father–she has no brothers, only one sister–made her a director. (*Parade,* October 10, 1976)

The writer clearly assumes that, had her father had a male heir, her talents would understandably never have been realized. Like the writer of the insurance ad discussed on page 63, this writer tacitly acknowledges the legitimacy of past discrimination. Many people bypass the question of whether women are able to perform effectively in the business world and concentrate instead on the question of whether such a public display of feminine talent is seemly or ladylike. This attitude is becoming socially, legally, and politically inexpedient, and no writer should make the mistake of assuming it is a widely shared view.

Other writers affect great surprise as they discover women are entirely capable of performing jobs formerly dominated by men. This "gee-whiz" tone of writing is a veiled insult because it assumes the accomplishments of the woman under discussion are flukes of nature and noteworthy because of their extreme improbability. This tone creeps into many "first woman in the job" articles. Any lead-in which ends with a question mark should be examined for this tone. Although the headline for the next example maintains that "femininity presents no hindrance for a standards technician," the lead paragraph suggests otherwise:

> In Onan's Standards department, there are seven Industrial Engineering technicians who are currently at work establishing computerized standards in Manufacturing departments. Their names are Paul, Bob, Don, Gary, Marland, Ken, and Joyce. Joyce? (Onan Corporation *Onannewsbrief,* June-July 1976)

A third dangerous practice is attributing motivation to working women as a group. The following passage ignores the fact that 13 percent of all families in 1975 were headed by women and that 45 percent of all families below the poverty line were headed by women:

> . . .Most women, however, do not want to enter the work force at the expense of men. To do so would be to shift to themselves the burden of financial responsibility for the family, and they don't want to assume it entirely. (*Management Review,* May 1974)

The reasons women work are too diverse for glib "explanations" of their motives. Elitist assumptions such as the belief that all families are headed by married men whose wives, if they work, do so only for "pin money" or for self-enrichment have vicious consequences for women working out of stark necessity, and the "pin money" myth trivializes the contributions of all working women. If you wonder why a woman went into a particular line of work, ask her and quote her accurately.

Perhaps the most harmful myth is the one which presumes that women either do not want or cannot handle job responsibility. The underlying assumption is that the truly responsible woman is at home caring for her children. This myth constitutes double jeopardy for the woman who is the sole support of her children. One communicator dealt with the issue directly in the *Cabot Chronicle:*

> . . .Ron Burleson, Personnel and Safety Manager at Tuscola, commented that women's roles have changed radically there in the past year.

> "When the first woman was hired in the plant in July 1975," he said, "there was little reaction among the men. Some remarks were made, but we had no real problems because the women didn't want special treatment. They wanted the chance to do a good job and to earn a good salary with good benefits."
>
> Lee Ruphard, a Day Laborer in the siltet plant, agrees. *With three children to support, she appreciates the money and the benefits.* She operates a fork lift to unload 120,000-pound ore cars and does other odd jobs as required. (Cabot Corporation *Chronicle*, July 1976)

We are living in a time of great social change. The accelerating rate of change makes any reliance on past myths and stereotypes particularly dangerous. As a communicator you describe your company and its people in the midst of this change. When you write about women, you can be sure of avoiding out-moded sexist language and presumptions if you keep two general rules in mind: you should not insult women gratuitously and you cannot exclude them. Women are a part of today's business world. Your company's publications can and should reflect this fact in a fair and objective manner. A woman employee who received the following invitation to the company picnic might wonder whether she was really welcome:

> You and your immediate family are cordially invited to attend the 1976 COMPANY FAMILY BASKET PICNIC on Saturday. . . . One of the main objectives of our company picnic is to bring together employees and their families on a social basis so we can all become better acquainted and meet the *wives* and

> children we talk about at work but seldom have a chance to meet. . . .

An elite group of working women may have housekeepers, but not a single working woman has a wife. Your organization undoubtedly contains many women; acknowledge this by writing about them in an objective way.

Sources Cited

1. Spock, Benjamin. "How My Ideas About Women Have Changed." *Redbook.* November 1973.

2. Blackstone, William. *Commentaries on the Laws of England.* Dobb's Ferry, New York: Oceana Publications, 1966.

3. Westside Women's Committee. *"He" is not "She."* P.O. Box 24D20, Village Station, Los Angeles, CA 90024.

4. Miller, Casey and Smith, Kate. *Words and Women: New Language in New Times*. New York: Anchor Press, Doubleday and Company, 1976.

5. Orovan, Mary. *Humanizing English*. Mary Orovan, 130 East 18th Street, New York, New York 10003.

6. Kucera, Henry and Francis, W. Nelson. *Computational Analysis of Present-Day American English.* Providence, R.I.: Brown University Press, 1967.

7. Mertz, Maia Pank. "Popular Culture and the Social Construction of Reality." *English Education*. Fall 1976.

8. "Our account executives: a seasoned staff serving a limited clientele." Oppenheimer & Co. Inc. One New York Plaza, New York, New York.

9. "The Continuing Engineer." *Engineering Education News*. November 1976.

10. Burton, Dwight. "Relaxing with Back-to-Basics." *English Journal*. November 1976.

11. Corea, Gena. "Frankly Feminist." *Media Report to Women*, January 1, 1975.

12. LeGuin, Ursula. "Winter's King." *The Wind's Twelve Quarters*. New York: Bantam Books, 1975.

13. *Guidelines for Equal Treatment of the Sexes in McGraw-Hill Book Company Publications.* McGraw-Hill, New York, New York.

14. Salk, Lee. *Preparing for Parenthood*. New York: David McKay Company, 1974.

15. Scofield, Sandra. "Montana: Call in Neighbor." *Ms*. January 1977.

16. Killian, Ray A. *Human Resource Management: An ROI Approach*. New York: AMACOM, 1976.

17. Laurence, Patricia. "Error's Endless Train: Why Students Don't Perceive Error." *Journal of Basic Writing*. Spring 1975.

18. Schwartz, John L. "Judge Riddel remembered for nailing welfare cheater." Arizona *Republic*. October 18, 1976.

19. "Industrial Communication Lives," *Communication Notes*. August 1976.

20. "What your mother never told you about insurance." Nationwide Insurance advertisement.

21. "Meet the Crescent, Oregon, Volunteer Fire Department." Martin Marietta Corporation advertisement.

22. Shapiro, Benson P. and Posner, Ronald S. "Making the Major Sale." *Harvard Business Review*. March-April 1976.

23. "Minor Memos." *Wall Street Journal*. December 31, 1976.

24. *Job Title Revisions to Eliminate Sex- and Age-Referent Language from the Dictionary of Occupational Titles* (3rd ed.). Manpower Administration. U.S. Department of Labor, 1975.

NOTES

NOTES

As summer gave way to autumn, the high hopes for a South American odyssey evaporated. Apparently neither Ward, nor the Lecturer on Toxicology, nor Clemens could scrape up the money. He would get no kick from cocaine. Sam seethed, and labored on for nothing in the third-story shop.

But one day he struck it rich in the most hackneyed, banal, cartoon-strip manner imaginable.

He was trudging along the main street in Keokuk one bitter morning in October, fighting an early swirl of dry snow, when a rectangular scrap of paper fluttered past his eyes and flattened against the wall of a house. Sam peeled it off and examined it. It was a fifty-dollar bill—"the only one I had ever seen, and the largest assemblage of money I had ever seen in one spot." To be sure, it was more than triple the $16 that the Campbellites had brought into the Hannibal shop.

Astonishingly enough, Sam advertised his literal windfall in the local newspapers. (Not everything he did foretold the twentieth century.) Perhaps even more astonishingly still, after four days, not a solitary Iowa soul had responded to claim the money. On the fifth day, it struck Sam that virtue had its limits. ("Truth is the most valuable thing we have," he later wrote. "Let us economize it."[20]) He bought a ticket to St. Louis, and South America suddenly seemed possible after all.

His plan was to work his way down the Mississippi, making money where he could, and then, vaguely, to board a ship headed for Brazil. (He had only the foggiest notions about the location and nature of Brazil, and none at all about the lethal complexities of the Amazon.) Before he left town—and left Orion, once again, in the lurch—he struck a deal to write some humorous travel sketches back to the Keokuk *Daily Post*, for $5 each.

The first letter was postmarked October 18, 1856, from St. Louis, and it introduced the last pen name, and alter ego, that Sam would try out before he unveiled Mark Twain in Nevada in February 1863. This was the bumptious Iowa rustic Thomas Jefferson Snodgrass, just a little bit higher on the evolutionary scale than Simon Suggs. Heavily imitative of the old Southwestern traditions, his comic appeal depending on misspellings and grossly exaggerated ignorance, Snodgrass was not an especially clever creation in himself. As portrayed in Sam's first letter, Snodgrass and a companion go to the theater to see an actor named Nealy play *Julius Caesar.* Out of his element, Snodgrass decides to compete with the house orchestra by whipping out an old pocket comb and playing on it, taking "them one-hoss fiddlers down a peg and bring down the house, too."[21] The audience laughs, which gets Snodgrass riled:

> Darn my skin if I wasn't mad. I jerked off my coat and jumped at the little man and, says I, "You nasty, sneakin' degenerate great grandson of a ring-tailed monkey, I kin jest lam . . . "[22]

Snodgrass's summary of the plotline is as follows:

> At last it come time to remove Mr. Cesar from office . . . so all the conspirators got around the throne, and directly Cesar come steppin in, putting on as many airs as if he was mayor of Alexandria. Arter he had sot on the throne awhile they all jumped on him at once like a batch of Irish on a sick nigger.[23]

What was most useful about this and the two* other Snodgrass letters Sam wrote, perhaps, is that they earned him $5 apiece—his first fees for freelance writing.

That, and the fact that Snodgrass, however crude, is the literary "missing link" between Simon Suggs and Huckleberry Finn. As his skills deepened in the Nevada years and beyond, Mark Twain would keep writing in assumed human voices. But gradually he shed the arch misspellings and the clownish faked ignorance, and based his vernacular writing more and more on authentic figures of speech and the natural rhythms of spoken dialect. Thus when Huckleberry Finn finally emerged in 1884, he emerged with the capacities of the ironist and even the poet, without breaking the consistency of his character—qualities to which Suggs and his generation could never aspire.

Sam was restless. St. Louis could not hold him. Suddenly the need to make money and head off for the unknown overwhelmed him. He stayed only about a week, boarding with Jane and Pamela's family. In mid-October he threw himself into the slow journey upriver to Keokuk again, for the sole purpose of looking in on the editor at the *Post* and bargaining for more money for further Snodgrass letters. The next day he was heading back downstream, to Quincy. There he boarded a train for the two hundred-mile trip to Chicago. He made connections south to Indianapolis, and finally, around October 24, he arrived in Cincinnati. He landed a printing job there, at T. Wrightson & Co., where he worked through the spring of 1857.

---

*The scholar Minnie Brashear discovered four additional Snodgrass letters in the *New Orleans Crescent* beginning January 21, 1861, but their authorship by Clemens is doubtful. This character is called Quintus Curtius Snodgrass, and his voice is not vernacular, but pretentious and literary.

Mark Twain never wrote much about those months in Cincinnati. By all inferences they were lonely and fitful: boardinghouses and drudgework through a long winter. Hoarding his pay. Two more Snodgrass letters issued from there to be printed in the Keokuk paper.

Finally, on April 15, 1857, Sam Clemens made the break from his landlocked life. More decisively, in the short run at least, than leaving Hannibal, he left the world of safe employment, the world of dry ground, and hit the river for adventure. At age twenty-one, he booked passage on the steamboat *Paul Jones,* out of Cincinnati, bound westward on the Ohio and then down the Mississippi for New Orleans. His plan, manifestly, was to find a seagoing ship that would get him to South America. Unfortunately for his Amazon dreams and Henry Clemens, and fortunately for American literature, the pilot of the *Paul Jones* had a sore foot and a malleable turn of mind. By the time the boat docked at New Orleans eleven days later, Sam had talked his way onto the texas deck, had taken over most of the steering, and had become convinced that his real destiny was to steer riverboats for a living.

The pilot's name was Horace Bixby. A small sturdy man of thirty-one when Sam Clemens made his intrusion, he had a prominent nose, a firmly set mouth, and hair brushed all the way across his head from a low part. He would survive a steamboat explosion near New Madrid, Missouri in 1858, pilot heroically for the Union flotilla during the Civil War, achieve greatness in his trade, and outlive Mark Twain by two years, dying a few months after the *Titanic* sank in 1912, in a St. Louis suburb. Thus he lived to see the full effusion and even share the celebrityhood unleashed by his indulgence of the small, drawling young man suddenly at his elbow on the Ohio River, where the young man was now for the second time being conceived.

In Mark Twain's semifictionalized remembrance of his first encounter with Bixby, he retained the affect of a boy, rather than a twenty-one-year-old man. Once the "ancient tub" is under way downriver, for instance, he was overcome with a boy's exultant sense of being a king, "bound for mysterious lands and distant climes."

> . . . when we stopped at villages and wood-yards, I could not help lolling carelessly upon the railings of the boiler-deck to enjoy the envy of the country boys on the bank. If they did not seem to discover me, I presently sneezed to attract their attention, or moved to a position where they could not help seeing me. And as soon as I knew they saw me I gaped and stretched, and gave other signs of being mightily bored with travelling.[24]

A good deal more revealing than that set-piece bit of cuteness, perhaps, is his revelation a few paragraphs later of his delight in the *language* that washed over him on board—the rich, profane vernacular of the rivermen:

> "Here, now, start that gang-plank for'ard! Lively, now! *What*'re you about! Snatch it! *Snatch* it! There! There! Aft again! aft again! Don't you hear me? Dash it to dash! Are you going to *sleep* over it! '*Vast* heaving. 'Vast heaving, I tell you! Going to heave it clear astern? WHERE're you going with that barrel! *For'ard* with it 'fore I make you swallow it, you dash-dash-dash-*dashed* split between a tired mud-turtle and a crippled hearse-horse!"
>
> I wished I could talk like that.[25]

He could, of course, and did; ultimately such a passage is mimetic Twain, talking. The passage, and many others like it in *Life on the Mississippi*, suggest that Sam Clemens's attraction to the river derived as much from the human language peculiar to the river culture as from the river itself. (Indisputably, he heard money talking as well: river-pilots' "princely" salaries, up to $250 a month, were legendary in the country then, and Sam would forever be drawn to the prospect of the big payday.) River and language, in any case, would soon be conjoined in his creative consciousness. His language would flow like a river; his books, never tightly plotted, would seem instead to follow some mysterious course of their own making—shifting channels, eroding certain boundaries, flooding at times, running nearly dry at others, spilling over capriciously onto the high ground. As for the river itself, he learned to "read" it, and the river became a wonderful book, "a book that was a dead language to the uneducated . . . but which told its mind to me without reserve, delivering its most cherished secrets as clearly as if it had uttered them with a voice."[26]

Twain even seems to drop a prophetic reprimand, a paragraph later, to the literary clinicians of the century to come. An overemphasis of the river as text, he warns, has hazards of its own to give:

> Now when I had mastered the language of this water and had come to know every trifling feature that bordered the great river as familiarly as I knew the letters of the alphabet, I had made a valuable acquisition. But I had lost something, too. I had lost something which could never be restored to me while I lived. All the grace, the beauty, the poetry had gone out of the majestic river![27]

But all that mastery, and all that loss, were yet to come. His first agenda aboard the *Paul Jones* was to somehow meet the pilot and get control of the wheel.

Horace Bixby himself recalled to the biographer Paine that his first awareness of Sam Clemens was as a voice—a "slow, pleasant voice" that spoke up one sunlit day from behind his shoulder as he steered the boat along toward St. Louis. The voice wanted to know whether Bixby would like to teach a young man the river. Bixby thought he wouldn't like it at all. But the voice itself caught his attention. "What makes you pull your words that way?" he remembered asking; and the answer came back, more slowly still and in some way irresistibly comic, "You'll have to ask my mother. She pulls hers, too."[28]

Then the owner of the voice—"a rather slender, loose-limbed young fellow with a fair, girlish complexion and a great tangle of auburn hair"[29]—took a seat on the visitors bench a few feet from the wheel and asked Bixby whether he knew the Bowen brothers. Bixby said he did; he'd supervised Will Bowen's first steering. "A mighty good boy, too. Had a Testament in his pocket when he came aboard; in a week's time he had it swapped for a deck of cards."[30] The auburn-haired youth replied that Will, Sam, and Bart had been schoolmates of his in Hannibal. Bixby asked him whether he drank, gambled, swore, or chewed. The young man replied that he did not. Well, qualify that: in terms of swearing, "Not for amusement; only under pressure."[31] It occurred to Bixby that he could use a little relief for his sore foot. He sat down and let the young man take the wheel. "Keep her as she is—toward that lower cottonwood snag."[32] The Amazon receded; the Mississippi swelled.

It was in New Orleans that Sam launched his plea to Bixby for a position as an apprentice, or cub pilot. Before he did that, he apparently made some last inquiries around town about whether it would be possible to make a boat connection to the Amazon. (It wasn't.) He and Bixby agreed on terms: $500, of which $100 must be paid in advance. (In *Life on the Mississippi,* Mark Twain suggests that the bargaining occurred during a "three-day seige" en route downriver from Cincinnati.) The *Paul Jones* left New Orleans for St. Louis on April 30, where Sam set about rounding up the money. He called on his wealthy distant cousin James Clemens again, and again left without satisfaction: "Before I got to the subject he was wailing about having to pay $25,000 taxes in N.Y. City—said it makes a man poor! So I didn't ask him."[33] Sam was luckier with William A. Moffett, Pamela's husband. He secured a loan, presented it as the deposit, closed the agreement with Bixby, and on May 22, he and his mentor were steaming back down to New Orleans aboard the *Crescent City,* his career as a riverboat pilot contractually underway.

The river distance between St. Louis and New Orleans—Bixby's essential territory—was thirteen hundred miles. Every mile bore its distinct feature: river width, river depth, location of the channel, the presence of underwater snags, rocks, shoals, and previously sunken watercraft, including giant steamers. Sam's first revelation regarding the immensity of his chosen trade was that he would have to memorize the river. Mile by mile. His second revelation was that his education had begun before he knew it—Bixby's habit of mentioning landmarks to him on that first downriver passage had not been a matter of idle chitchat. Mark Twain made great semifictional sport of this—James Cox has likened the episodes to a series of vaudeville acts—in his reminiscences:

> Presently he turned on me and said:—
>
> "What's the name of the first point above New Orleans?"

> I was gratified to be able to answer promptly, and I did. I said I didn't know.[34]

But it wasn't a matter of sport at the time. Sam's third revelation was that he had to memorize the river in both directions: memorize twenty-six hundred miles of river, that is; or, more accurately, memorize two separate rivers, given not only that the visual prospect was utterly different, but also that a boat behaved quite differently with the flow behind it than it did breasting the current.

His fourth revelation was that he had to retain a mental image of the *shape* of the river, the river entire, for there were times when the river's particularized contours could not matter. As Bixby explained: "It is all there is left to steer by on a very dark night. Everything else is blotted out and gone." That was the easy part. "But mind you, it has n't the same shape in the night that it has in the daytime."[35]

The fifth and final revelation, following quickly on the fourth, was that the imprinted shape of the river entire did not matter ultimately anyway, given that the river entire never sustained itself, as Heraclitus saw, from one second to the next. The river's banks were constantly caving in, new channels constantly spilling across dry land, new islands constantly being formed and obliterated, and land that had been Missouri property one day reemerging as a part of Illinois the next.

These revelations may well have been fictionalized compressions of more subtle and complex processes by which Sam Clemens learned the pilot's trade. But to the extent that they are true—and their irreducible truth has not been contradicted by scholarship—they suggest an elemental conversion in Sam's lifelong comprehension of the river.

The river, it was turning out, was never exactly what it appeared to be. The river was a chimera, a memory.

The river that he had known since childhood—the greatest constant in his oft-disrupted life, more enduring even than his family—this river, the Father of Waters—did not, in certain ways of thinking of it, exist. Certainly it did not flow into or out of a world that could be understood in terms of the rational, the predictable, the sunlit. The river was a dream, dark and mystical, forever evanescent, yet forever in terrible control of the lives of mortal men. The dream was dangerous—dangerous water; that's what the leadsman's cry of "mark twain" essentially meant: two marks, two fathoms, twelve feet, the bottom rushing up from the depths to scrape and threaten and capsize the craft. The danger of running aground was his most searing association with the cry of "*Mark* twain":

> Then came the leadsman's sepulchral cry:—
>
> "D-e-e-p four!"
>
> Deep four in a bottomless crossing! The terror of it took my breath away.
>
> "M-a-r-k three! . . . M-a-r-k three . . . Quarter less three! . . . Half twain!"
>
> This was frightful! I seized the bell-ropes and stopped the engines.
>
> "Quarter twain! Quarter twain! *Mark* twain!"
>
> I was helpless. I did not know what in the world to do. I was quaking from head to foot, and I could have hung my hat on my eyes, they stuck out so far.
>
> "Quarter *less* twain! Nine and a *half*!"
>
> . . . My hands were in a nervous flutter. I could not ring a bell intelligibly with them. I flew to the speaking-tube and shouted to the engineer,—

> "Oh, Ben, if you love me, *back* her! Quick, Ben! Oh, back the immortal *soul* out of her!"[36]

The consummating irony here is that Sam's peril is itself an illusion, his terror a construct of Horace Bixby's mentoring strategies. The "crossing"* in this incident was not shallow at all, a fact that Sam had already committed to memory. Bixby had instructed the leadsman to call out false depths as a way of testing Sam's courage and his confidence in his own knowledge of the river.

What it may have done, in some incremental way (along with a thousand other episodes of unreliable perception), is reinforce an abiding metaphor in Mark Twain's life and work: that things are seldom what they seem, reality and illusion being deeply intertwined. The river was awash in dualities; it ceaselessly reinvented itself; it switched identities; it was its own twin, upstream and down. Its deceptively sweet currents masked deeply encoded messages. Its many interconnected stretches, running fast and slow, straight and curved, were dialects that needed close attention. Wreckage lay strewn below the surface. Danger was the only constant of life on the phantasmal Mississippi; that is to say, of life. And the only question to be asked, in retrospect, was: *Which Was the Dream?*

---

*A "crossing" was a lateral movement by a pilot seeking to maneuver his boat from one side of the river to the other in search of the deepest water. Crossings were frequent, and called forth the pilot's greatest navigational skills and most intimate knowledge of the river's varying depths.

Fifteen

"I think a pilot's memory is about the most wonderful thing in the world."

The dangers of the river are curiously muted in Mark Twain's writings. The man who would come, enraged, to forage through the dark side of nearly everything else of value in his life—his friends, his work, his nation, his god, his faith in man, even (in "The Mysterious Stranger" and "The Man That Corrupted Hadleyburg") his edenic hometown—this same embittered man would never profane the sanctity of the Mississippi. In *Huckleberry Finn,* most of the perils that confront Huck and Jim are the perils of dry land: the feuding Shepardsons/Grangerfords, the murderous Colonel Sherburn, the predatory con artists who come aboard the raft. On the river, they are safe. Even in the latter chapters of *Life on the Mississippi*, the "unnerved terror" and the "miasma of negativity" noticed by critics such as Richard Bridgman[1] have as their referents not the river so much as the America and the world that surround it.

In fact, something like the reverse was the case. While inland America was anything but a peaceable kingdom, its rivers seemed to attract its roughest, most predatory citizens. From Mike Fink and his fellow flatboatmen onward, riverways and their shores were conduits for crime, carnality, and confidence men. All the reckless and violent impulses of the frontier coalesced on the river, where the action was.

Twain's wish for a myth of the river as semi-divine obliged him to avert his gaze from these impulses. (This wish bears intriguing parallels to the prophylactic wishes his daughter, close friends, and biographer nursed for his own posthumous reputation.) His blindered ardency is nowhere more concisely expressed than in the four-paragraph chapter 21 of *Life on the Mississippi,* the one entitled "A Section of My Biography." This is the transitional chapter that conjoins the earlier sections, most of them previously published in *The Atlantic Monthly* in 1875, with the new material that Twain gathered upon his return to the river in 1882.

"I supposed—and hoped—that I was going to follow the river the rest of my days, and die at the wheel when my mission was ended," he writes. "But by and by the war came, commerce was suspended, my occupation was gone."[2] He disposes of the intervening twenty-one "slow-drifting" years of his life in seventy-four words:

> I had to seek another livelihood. So I became a silver miner in Nevada; next, a newspaper reporter; next, a gold miner, in California; next, a reporter in San Francisco; next, a special correspondent in the Sandwich Islands; next, a roving correspondent in Europe and the East; next, an instructional torch-bearer on the lecture platform; and, finally, I became a scribbler of books, and an immovable fixture among the other rocks of New England.[3]

"Let us," he writes at the end of this, "resume now."

But resume what? The four years (April 1857 to May 1861) that Sam spent as a pilot on the Mississippi, by implication the happiest of his life, are also among his least revealed. Only fourteen of his letters are preserved from that time, including four written during his apprentice-pilot period, and two of his notebooks, largely devoted to river minutiae but also containing a little melancholy poetry and some exercises in the French language. Inferential evidence suggests that he became a highly skilled pilot (contrary to the self-lampooning persona that he created in memoirs). But the evidence also suggests that the river culture he cherished was far from the elegant, bucolic, and lighthearted realm that Mark Twain immortalized in his books.

In fact the evidence suggests that in steamboating Sam Clemens descended into a dark demimonde indeed: a substrata of American materialism, greed, vice, and corruption that rivaled and foreshadowed any measure of commercial mendacity the late twentieth century had to offer.

"An economic reality hideous with cut-throat tactics," the historian Bernard DeVoto has called it—"an American commerce without conscience, responsibility or control."[4] The great alabastrine sidewheelers and sternwheelers that crowded the river in that thirty-five-year era have been enshrined in the country's souvenir-ashtray art and in popular memory as "floating palaces," "multi-tiered wedding cakes," "Turkish minarets." In fact they were gilding, as false and mannered as the fantasy architecture coating a twentieth-century shopping mall. As false, and far more dangerous. What the gilding obfuscated was an ongoing tournament of rapacious profiteering, bribery, unenforced standards of safety, and, all too frequently, abrupt, fiery mass death.

The steamboats, owned by wealthy individuals and small companies, were all going after a lucrative but finite universe of commercial freight: cotton, livestock, hay, corn, turpentine, dry goods, light machinery, imported European wines and perfumes, and other luxuries from the docks at New Orleans. Chockablock with the commodities was the human cargo: merchants, touring folk, immigrants, farmers, poor laborers who slept on the main deck; slaves and their masters en route from one condition of bondage to another; gamblers, swindlers, pimps, and prostitutes. "Floating brothels" was a common description that never quite made it to the souvenir ashtrays. "Floating casinos" would have served just as well, and the perfumed, broad-hatted "riverboat gambler" indeed became enshrined in the nation's folklore.

There were few rules, and the owners, who did not themselves typically travel by riverboat, were not especially ardent to play by those few. Often, the captains, pilots, and crew either matched this cynicism or were, at crucial moments, too drunk or absorbed in racing another craft to care. And yet a rough law-and-order system prevailed. Thieves, rapists, brawlers, whores, card-sharks, and other familiar troublemakers could find themselves hauled up before a makeshift jury of their fellow passengers; if "convicted," they faced flogging, being tossed onto the wilderness shore, or running the gauntlet. The ultimate jurist on a riverboat was the captain, and the captain's dispensation could be primitive and terrifying.

These scabrous facts of steamboat life were camouflaged, to some extent, by surface packaging. Superficially, the great boats could be as ornate and rococo as a theme restaurant; their grace-notes wowed the rubes and the paying customers. Sam Clemens of Hill Street in Hannibal was plausibly dazzled by the *Crescent City's* long, gilded saloon, its oil paintings, its prism-fringed chandeliers. He was understandably in awe of another big New Orleans boat's "bright, fanciful 'cuspadores'"[sic], the sumptuous glass temple of its pilot house, and its white-aproned black servant who brought tarts, ices, and coffee to the lounging pilots during mid-watch. But Mark Twain is effectively silent about the pervasive, lethal cost-cutting and the often pitiless attitudes that these showy appointments concealed.

The overall construction of the boats, for example, was often shockingly slapdash. Steamers of up to 350 feet in length—the distance from home plate to the outfield wall in a typical baseball stadium—were made of thin, resinous, dry timber and whitened with turpentine-rich paint that responded incandescently to sparks. This was the experience of the *Ben Sherrod* in 1837, among many others. Headed upriver to Louisville, her captain and crew firing the furnaces in an effort to outrace another boat, the *Ben Sherrod*'s superstructure received one enflamed ember too many. Oblivious to the safety of the two hundred passengers, the captain ordered the ignited boat to continue its upriver surge. By the time the tiller ropes had burned, making steering impossible, the engineer had fled his post and the boat was out of control. Soon the flames had reached the cargo, which included several casks of brandy and several others of gunpowder. When these exploded, the boilers went up. Survivors recalled

> [t]he screams of men, women and children [that] pierced the air for miles around while in the bright light that went up from the waters the hanging forms of the poor wretches as they clung convulsively to the burning sides of the boat struck the deepest anguish into the hearts of spectators.[5]

Another steamboat, the *Alton,* churned upriver past the stricken boat, but the pilot was in a hurry and did not stop. In fact an investigating committee found that his craft had run over many people flailing about in the water, and drowned still others with its waves. In all, about 150 of the 200 were lost.

The boats' similarly thin flat bottoms offered little resistance to snags, rocks, or the jutting structures of their sunken counterparts. In 1851 the *John Adams*, headed upriver, struck a snag about 200 miles below Memphis. The impact split the boat's hull in two; it sank almost instantly, drowning 113 of the 230 people on board.[6]

Bursting boilers were perhaps the major source of catastrophe. The *Moselle,* for example, paid a dear price in 1838 for its captain's thought to put on a splendid show of dashing past the Cincinnati waterfront. He overheated the fires a bit and made the regrettable mistake of loading down the safety valve. The resulting explosion afforded Cincinnatians the spectacle of a steam-and-smoke cloud that rose several hundred feet in the air, along with debris and fragments of many human bodies.[7]

The thing about the boilers was that no one could figure out for the longest time—decades, in fact—just what it was that made them explode.

In all, some 995 accidents were reported on the Western rivers in the years 1811–51 alone—the heyday of such occurrences. The average lifespan of a riverboat was four to five years.

The conflagrations, explosions, and snaggings were hardly secret; the newspapers covered them lavishly. Yet virtually no depiction of the causative aggression, the cynicism, or the resulting horror appears in Mark Twain's writings about the river, in fiction or memoir. ("Racing was royal fun," he wrote fatuously in a chapter devoted to that deadly pastime.[8]) His typic Victorian reticence might explain the silence regarding the prostitution that flourished there. But sexuality aside, he was never hesitant to limn human avarice and cruelty in his other books and essays: the trigger-happy psychopaths and the opium dens of the West, the macabre dueling societies of Heidelberg, the savagery of King Leopold of the Congo, the greed of the plutocratic robber barons, the iniquities of the Christian God, a thousand other examples. It is the river alone that he held, for the most part, sacrosanct.

It was not a matter of a faulty memory. To be sure, Twain's memory was, in many human ways, flawed. As he aged, he developed an absentmindedness about names, dates, and events. Much of this, however, was less a fading of his faculties than a kind of psychic editing; he was forever revising his life to make it even more interesting and melodramatic than it had been. In most important ways, his recall was extraordinary. His reproduction of human speech, while nearly always revised by his poetic instincts for what the speaker *should have* said, was one of the wonders of the nineteenth century's artistic universe; it prefigured and enabled the great stream of American Southern dialecticians to come, including Faulkner, O'Connor, Welty, and Wolfe, and perhaps even such Yankees as Fitzgerald, O'Hara, and Salinger.

His memory was trained on the river, by Bixby's constant goadings. "To know the Old and New Testaments by heart . . . is no extravagant mass of knowledge," he liked to claim, "compared to a pilot's massed knowledge of the Mississippi and his marvellous [sic] facility in the handling of it."[9]

One possible explanation for this great vacuum in his critical attention is that Mark Twain was complicit in the corruptions of the river as he was complicit in no other topic for his moral satire. (The Wall Street plutocracy, which helped rescue him from bankruptcy in his old age, may be the exception.) The Mississippi River steamboat trade was about money and what money would buy, and Clemens spent his life following money. Along with his fellow pilots, he well appreciated the connection between money and memory: "At the time that wages soared so high on the Missouri River, my chief, Mr. Bixby, went up there and learned more than a thousand miles of that stream with an ease and rapidity that were astonishing."[10] Among the first things he noticed about the grand pilots (as an envious cub) were their polished silk hats, their elaborate shirt fronts, their diamond breastpins, their kid gloves, and their patent-leather boots. Before long, he was showing up on deck in patent-leather boots, blue serge coats, white duck trousers and boldly striped shirts, a French reader or a copy of Tom Paine's *Common Sense* tucked under his arm. And he was "dissipating" with his master Bixby on ten-dollar New Orleans dinners of sheepshead fish, oysters, birds, and mushrooms,[11] washed down presumably with something other than Mississippi ice-water.

As an apprentice and later as a pilot, he found himself at the epicenter of the entire system of money, goods, power, pleasure; he and his skilled, memory-saturated peers at the big spiked wheels were literally what made it all run.

To criticize (or even to feel critical of) the steamboat culture from that vantage point would have been virtually self-negating. It would have been comparable to a truck driver of a later time speaking out against the highway lobby or the moral outrages of driving cross-country on amphetamines. Truck drivers typically sentimentalize their calling, encoding their attitude toward it in the self-lionizing verses of country-western songs. "Old Times on the Mississippi," Twain's series of reminiscences in the Atlantic that form the first half of his 1883 book, are to some limited extent the extended-prose ancestors of the Flying Burrito Brothers hit "Six Days on the Road (And I'm Gonna Make It Home Tonight)."

He reaped another substantial dividend from his river-years, one that he did not hesitate to describe in terms of capital gain:

> I am to this day profiting somewhat by that experience; for in that brief, sharp schooling, I got personally and familiarly acquainted with about all the different types of human nature that are to be found in fiction, biography, or history. . . . When I find a well-drawn character in fiction or biography, I generally take a warm personal interest in him, for the reason that I have known him before—known him on the river.[12]

He found there, in other words, the mother-lode of human character: character even more diverse and abject and vivid than he was to encounter in Nevada, the land of the mother lode itself. On the river he found characters who (as has been said of the characters in *The Great Gatsby,* who share subtle affinities) were constantly in the act of self-revelation. Illusion always existed in tension with the hard facts. River characters were blunt prolific talkers, for the most part, giving to Twain's ear the stripped-down, high-velocity pitch that he hurled into the thick upholstery of American letters. River characters talked in jargon, in a thousand jargons: pilots, roustabouts, officers, hustlers, slaves, refined women, unrefined women, Europeans, mystics, soldiers, killers, the clergy. Collectively they offered up a constant bonanza of language and predicament.

Sam may or may not have written it all down—there is little evidence that he did—but he invested it somehow, and when the time came to draw interest, it was all there, waiting. The effect of those years, as DeVoto said, is visible in Mark Twain's perception of the human animal. He imported those effects off the river and into his books. *Tom Sawyer* may have been possible without the river years, but certainly not *Huckleberry Finn, Pudd'nhead Wilson, The Gilded*

Age, The American Claimant, any number of his essays and sketches—to say nothing of the vast and enigmatic *Life on the Mississippi.* T. S. Eliot was right in calling him a servant of the river-god.

Little wonder, then, that Mark Twain might have wished to spare the river the revelations of its sweet sinfulness—or his own sweet sinfulness—on the printed page.

But there is a final reason why Mark Twain might have wanted to leave the darker reaches of the Mississippi River undisturbed in his many literary revisitings, a reason connected to the final sorrow of his youth, a sorrow spawned of fire and water, fire and water out of kilter, fire and water bringing death.

Sixteen

"... my darling, my pride, my glory, my all ..."

Ripe New Orleans put him in mind of death. It seemed to belong to some other order of things, a city at the end of the river, where the vital current dissipated finally into the infinite vastness. A city of masks and funerals and above-ground cemeteries, "cities of the dead"; of Catholic symbols and bawdy celebrations; a place where Europeans and Africans, slave and free, commingled and made a dense compost of mysticism—New Orleans was a hive of voodoo priests and fortune-tellers, of conjure women who got in touch with the other side.

He prowled the teeming precincts each time his boat docked there, the end of the line. The cemeteries, with their exposed vaults,[1] caught his imagination above everything else. He marveled at them in a letter to Annie Taylor on June 1, after he and Bixby had disembarked the town's namesake boat, the *Crescent City*. He pouted a little about her lack of correspondence, then described his visit to the lushly vegetative French market, with its "pretty pyramids of fresh fruit." Finally, he dwelt on his visit to one of the many distinctive cemeteries in the heart of town: "a veritable little city, for they *bury* everybody *above* ground here." He told Annie about the tiered vaults, twelve feet high and laid off in straight streets, each tier containing several marble tombs where the coffins were inserted endways. "I noticed one beautiful white marble tomb, with a white lace curtain in front of it, under which, on a little shelf, were vases of fresh flowers, several little statuettes, and cups of water. . . . It looked so pretty."* He spent half an hour absorbed in the chameleons that scurried along the tombs, "strange animals, to change their clothes so often!" He teased and prodded one of them under a fresh leaf, "and he turned the brightest green color you ever saw!"

Twenty-five years later, revisiting New Orleans for the composition of his great river book, Mark Twain would not find the cemeteries quite so enchanting. The chameleons were merely reptilian little fly-catchers; their changes of color "are not up to the creature's reputation." He curled his lip at the "immortelles," or black-linen wreaths, that "pious hands" had placed on the tombs of their beloved: "you just hang it up, and there you are; just leave it alone, it will take care of your grief for you, and keep it in mind better than you can; stands weather first-rate, and lasts like boiler-iron."[2] As for the corpses themselves, they gave off unhealthy gases and ought to have been cremated; one could burn a person for four or five dollars and get soap enough out of his ashes to foot the bill. The entire subject of graveyards he found "grotesque, ghastly, horrible."[3]

No letters from Sam survive, beyond the Annie Taylor one, for the next nine months. This was the most intensive period of his cub-piloting experience; he doubtless had little time for correspondence. He continued up and down the Mississippi under Bixby until July,

*Underground cemeteries in New Orleans were impossible, given the city ground's high-water table and frequent flooding, which guaranteed that coffins would be waterlogged. The forty-odd "cities of the dead" that still exist there, with their marbled facades and wrought-iron gatings, are world-famous tourist attractions.

then was assigned to a series of other pilots after Bixby decided to try the Missouri River. In his old age his reminiscences of this period call back happy times: moonlight dancing on the boiler-deck, daylight frolics, shipmates who were good-hearted and convivial.

Bixby returned in the fall for a couple of trips with Sam, and then, in November, reassigned him again, this time to a sumptuous boat named the *Pennsylvania,* piloted by a team that included a man named Brown. Each entity proved something other than it might at first have seemed.

The *Pennsylvania* was an elegant behemoth, a 486-ton sidewheeler built in 1854 to carry passengers and mail. River-trade reportage of the time praised its "beautiful proportions" and "magnificent style."[4] Yet for all its harmonious facade, the boat was, in terms of its relationship to its host economy, a predator; a kind of death's-head in disguise. It was owned not by an independent rogue-businessman of the classic antebellum stripe, but by a newer, more extractive sort of corporatized master: the St. Louis, Cairo, and New Orleans Railroad Line. Its function was to provide a river link to an emerging, competitive system of transportation. That system would, in the post–Civil War years, usurp the steamboat economy, vitiate its gaudy, sordid culture, and introduce the nation to a new form of rapacious capitalism. "The unholy train," Mark Twain would call it upon his 1882 return to the river, that ultimately made havoc with his beloved era.

Brown, too, was a figure apart—apart, even, from the hardheaded, cocky run of Mississippi riverboat pilots. It is interesting that "Brown" became a favored fictive name in Mark Twain's travel writings of the 1860s. In his newspaper letters from Hawaii, in his subsequent dispatches en route from California to New York, and in the essays from the *Quaker City* that formed the first draft of *The Innocents Abroad,*

"Brown" is an all-purpose dark-comic foil, a know-it-all evil twin who voices the less palatable of Twain's observations. In his first appearance in *Life on the Mississippi,* it is hard to tell William Brown from Twain's fictionalized device: He is a garrulous windbag who can remember absolutely everything, but understand virtually nothing.

But William Brown of the *Pennsylvania* emerges from stereotype in good time. He becomes as genuine an article as a bolt of lightning on a summer night over Hannibal, foreshadowing God's dark judgment. An "ignorant, stingy, malicious, snarling, fault-finding, mote-magnifying tyrant," as Twain excoriated him. On the evidence, a sadist, if not a psychopath.

Sam's first memorable experience aboard the *Pennsylvania* was a near-catastrophe. The boat collided with the *Vicksburg* a few miles above New Orleans within a couple of weeks after he came onboard. Its starboard wheelhouse knocked askew, it was placed in drydock for repairs that stretched over eleven weeks. Sam spent part of that time as a night watchman on the New Orleans levee. He may have traveled up to St. Louis for the Christmas holidays.

He was aboard the *Pennsylvania* when it left drydock and headed back upriver in February 1858. Again, he flirted with disaster, as he described in a letter to Orion and Mollie Clemens up in Iowa.[5] The Mississippi was clogged with ice. The *Pennsylvania* inched upriver, stopping frequently so the captain could send small sounding boats out to locate the shifting channel. Sam saw duty on several of these expeditions. He struggled along with his mates in the frigid waters, was nearly run over by the parent boat on one occasion; on another, was forced ashore on an island in rain and sleet; on another, labored in the yawl from 4 in the morning until 9:30 at night without benefit of a warming fire. "There was a thick coating of ice over men, yawl, ropes, and everything else," he told Orion and Mollie, "and we looked like rock-candy statuary."[6]

In the very next sentence he reported that he had drawn his younger brother Henry into employment on the *Pennsylvania.*

> Henry was doing little or nothing here [St. Louis], and I sent him to our clerk to work his way for a trip, by measuring woodpiles, counting coal boxes, and other clerkly duties, which he performed satisfactorily. He may go down with us again, for I expect he likes our bill of fare better than that of his boarding house.[7]

Henry was nineteen then. His life is mostly a closed book to history, save through his brother's observations. A photograph made probably in 1858, when he was nearing twenty, shows him ovalfaced, clean-shaven, and pompadoured, with perhaps a trace of baby-fat still in his cheeks. (Beside him, bearded haunted Orion looks positively soignee.) His mouth, not so wide as Sam's rather shapely and sensuous one, is faintly pursed, and his eyes, fixed and serious as they gaze past the camera, have caught the glint of the flash-powder. He is wearing a wide-lapeled coat and a badly knotted bow tie that is too large for his starched whitecollar.

He never traveled on his own; he stuck close to the family. Intelligent, inward, he seems content to have haunted libraries, met obligations, behaved responsibly. What external definition his life had seems mostly to have been supplied by Orion and Sam. Orion could always count on Henry for employment in his ragtag printshop enterprises; Sam, when he was around, would provide companionship, teasing, and the occasional well-aimed watermelon shell.

In the spring of 1858, Sam saw the chance to deepen the newfound friendship with Henry that had begun in Keokuk. Orion and Mollie had left Iowa for Tennessee with their daughter; Orion would study law and try (without luck) to unload the Tennessee land. Henry was more or less stranded in St. Louis, working odd jobs, living at a boarding house, keeping in touch with his sister and mother, who were living in the city.

Getting Henry a position on the *Pennsylvania* was Sam's way of offering the boy an entree to his own exotic world. It was the kind of goodwill gesture that Mark Twain would curse in his old age—or more precisely, the kind of gesture that he would come to behold as cursed.

Henry and Sam made six trips together, in all, aboard the *Pennsylvania.* While Sam continued his pilot's training under Brown, intellectual Henry labored as an unpaid "mud-clerk," hopping off the boat at obscure stops to receive freight, hoping for a promotion up the line of status, to chief clerk, perhaps, or purser.

That spring was at once a demonic and a romantic time for Sam. The despot Brown had worked up a hatred for him, a frothing, hysterical torrent of sarcasm and abuse that seemed to serve as a perverse hobby of his at the wheel. (Apparently Brown sensed a class difference between himself and this son of a slave-owner who had been to school.) His constant hazing and fault-finding etched its way into Sam's nighttime reveries: "I killed Brown every night for months; not in old, stale, commonplace ways, but in new and picturesque ones,—ways that were sometimes surprising for freshness of design and ghastliness of situation and environment."[8]

As if to compensate for this torture, Sam spent that spring and summer in love, and loving what vanished. He sent pressed orange leaves with his letters to Annie Taylor. He searched for Keokuk girls in the French market. Blue-serge'd, white-duck'd, he strutted constantly, on the lookout. And then, as if summoned by a conjure spell, on the New Orleans waterfront, "floating upon my enchanted vision," there was Laura Wright.

Or, perhaps, there was, in Mark Twain's overheated memory of that catastrophic season, simply a dream of Laura Wright.

His memoirs have him encountering this vision one summer night as he invited himself aboard the *John J. Roe,* whose fo'castle the *Pennsylvania's* stern lapped upon putting in at the docks. Sam had been a steersman aboard the *Roe*. He knew its easygoing, jolly crew; a kind of sprawling family, really, of well-off Indiana hayseeds who always had an entourage of larking friends aboard. Joining this circle "was like arriving home at the farmhouse after a long absence."[9]

Laura Wright was among the guests, a judge's daughter. His first glimpse of her staggered Sam, as had his first glimpse of Laura Hawkins/Becky Thatcher in Hannibal. Not quite fifteen, on her first visit away from Missouri, this Laura overwhelmed him with some redolence of home, of purity in this decadent demimonde, of his own fast-receding boyhood. She "had brought with her to these distant regions the freshness and the fragrance of her own prairies."[10] He seems to have sanctified her on the spot—she became his "instantly elected sweetheart"—and forty-eight years later spoke of her with undiminished lyric passion: He could see her still with perfect distinctness "in the unfaded bloom of her youth, with her plaited tails dangling from her young head and her white summer frock puffing about in the wind of that ancient Mississippi time."[11] The passion must have been dangerously real to him; no hint of Laura Wright appears in *Life on the Mississippi,* written while Olivia was still alive.

Sam made some time for her. "I was not four inches from that girl's elbow during our waking hours for the next three days." In his dreamy recall he turned the parting into a theatrical *grand jete*, worthy of Sir Walter Scott (or Erroll Flynn): "Then there came a sudden interruption. Zeb Leavenworth came flying aft shouting, 'The *Pennsylvania* is backing out.' I fled at my best speed . . . made a flying leap and just did manage to make the connection, and nothing to spare. My toes found room on the guard; my finger-ends hooked themselves upon the guard-rail, and a quartermaster made a snatch for me and hauled me aboard."[12] In the dream, it became the last time he ever saw her.

Scholars have kept a wary distance between themselves and Mark Twain's salving dream. They have sensed the writer's famous mythifying imagination at work. That leap from boat to boat has struck the scholarly mind as awfully . . . convenient. The biographer John Lauber has stated categorically that the *Roe* and the *Pennsylvania* did not tie up together on the New Orleans waterfront that spring,[13] although his footnotes provide no substantiation of that.

And yet a Laura Wright there most assuredly was. And if Sam was guilty of falsely placing her aboard the *Roe,* Laura suffered under the same delusion. In a letter to him nearly half a century on, she described a frightening episode on the *Roe's* subsequent upriver journey: The boat struck a snag; an evacuation was ordered; one of the pilots discovered that Laura was not among the passengers massed for rescue. Knocking on her stateroom door, Laura's uncle and a mate heard her reply "quite calmly" that something was the matter with her hoop skirt and she would not come out until she had repaired it. "She kept her word and came ashore at her leisure, completely dressed."[14]

An entry in Sam's own notebook, dated May 6, reads: "This date, 1858, parted from L. Who said 'We shall meet again 30 years from now.'"[15] But they never did. Sam wrote to her; her mother probably intercepted the letters. A New Orleans fortune-teller described Laura to him with amazing accuracy in 1861. He wrote to Orion about that encounter, but added that even though Laura would always fault him for the impasse, he would not be the first to speak. Hurt pride prevented him from closing the gap between them, as hurt pride had prevented Jane Lampton from coming forward to her true love.

Two aftershocks renewed the pain of Laura. The first occurred in 1880 when he received a worshipful letter from a schoolboy in Dallas named Wattie Bowser, who wrote that "Mr. Twain" was the great man with whom he would most like to change places—would Mr. Twain be willing to trade off with him and become a boy again? Wattie's postscript jolted Twain: "Our principal used to know you, when you were a little boy and she was a little girl, but I expect you have forgotten her, it was so long ago." The principal's name was Laura Dake—the former Laura Wright. The great author's response was passionate and torrential. Yes, he would change places, if he could "emerge from boyhood as a 'cub pilot' on a Mississippi boat and become a pilot, and remain one." He would stipulate an eternal summer, with the oleanders in bloom and the sugar cane green, and a crew that would never change . . . and never die.[16]

The second aftershock hit twenty-six years later, during his *Autobiography* dictations. Within a few days after Mark Twain had found himself thinking and talking about Laura once more, he was stunned to receive a letter from her—a "world-worn and trouble-worn widow of sixty-two."[17] She needed money; money for herself and for her disabled son, who was thirty-seven. He sent her a thousand dollars, and wailed at the fiendishness of the world.

It was in her return letter of thanks that Laura told Twain about the *Roe's* snagging and her hoop-skirt crisis.

Within a few weeks after his initial discovery of Laura, death reasserted itself in young Sam Clemens's thoughts, with a dream of Henry inside a metal coffin.

At least he remembered that he did. Once again, the mythmaking habits of the aging writer seem a likely explanation for this fantasy of foreshadowing—as do the tendencies of traumatized people to transpose images of a tragedy to a time before the event. But here again, evidence disallows easy rationalizing: Annie Moffett, Pamela's young daughter, later recalled that Sam had spoken of the dream the morning after it supposedly occurred.

The dream, if it happened, probably happened around the first of June. The two brothers were in St. Louis for a three-day layover—Sam lodging at the Moffett household, Henry sleeping onboard the boat so as to be ready for his early-morning duties. Mark Twain's reconstruction of the dream did not lack for particulars.

> . . . I had seen Henry a corpse. He lay in a metallic burial case. He was dressed in a suit of my clothing and on his breast lay a great bouquet of flowers, mainly white roses, with a red rose in the center. The casket stood upon a couple of chairs.

The dream was so real to Sam that he had finished dressing and walked toward the door of the sitting room where he thought the coffin to be before changing his mind about entering: "I thought I could not yet bear to meet my mother. I thought I would wait awhile and make some preparation for that ordeal."[18] Not until he had left the Moffett house and walked a full block outdoors did he comprehend that the image of the coffin had been a dream. "I can still feel something of the grateful upheaval of joy of that moment."[19] But he also felt a lingering doubt, so he dashed back to the house, bounded up the stairs and into the sitting room, "and was made glad again, for there was no casket there."[20]

Later that day the *Pennsylvania* left the port at St. Louis and steamed south for New Orleans.

It was on this voyage that the pilot William Brown turned his sadistic attentions from Sam to Henry Clemens.

The seeds of the confrontation were planted sometime in the morning of June 3. It would have been the beginning of high summer on the river; of hot days, long lingering twilights; of lightning-bugs and mosquitoes thickening the shoreline at night, and the river itself heavy with scent. On this morning the boat was passing along the bluffs of the state of Mississippi to the east, the grassy swamplands of Louisiana to the west. Brown was at the wheel. Sam was in the pilothouse with him. Henry stepped into view on the hurricane deck to relay an order from the boat's captain, John S. Klinefelter, to stop at a plantation a short distance downstream. A stiff wind was blowing and Brown, whom Twain recalled as being deaf but unwilling to acknowledge it, gave no indication that he had heard the boy's message. Sam, who had heard it, elected not to speak.

As the boat steamed past its requested stop, Klinefelter swung out on deck and gave the order to come about, adding, in Twain's recollection, "Did n't Henry tell you to land here?" Brown snapped that

Henry had appeared, but "He never said anything." The captain turned to Sam: "Did n't *you* hear him?"

Here was a horrifying dilemma for Sam. To contradict Brown would be to invite retribution from a dangerous enemy. In the compacted universe of the western riverboat of the 1850s, the pilot enjoyed a sovereignty as absolute, in proportion, as any person of power in America. Tradition held that not even a boat's captain, not even the owner himself, could preempt a pilot's authority once the boat was under steam and the pilot had control of the wheel. On the other hand, to deny that he had heard Henry's message would be a bald betrayal of his brother. In a moment as fraught with moral significance as Huck Finn's decision to lie about Jim and "go to hell," Sam opted for the truth—and consigned himself, over the torments of his lifetime, to the same hot place. He said: "Yes, sir."

Brown's instant retort was: "Shut your mouth! You never heard anything of the kind."[21]

The inevitable payback came an hour later. Mark Twain put the location at a stretch on the Mississippi called Eagle Bend, near Pawpaw Island, about eighteen miles upriver from Vicksburg.[22] Henry entered the pilothouse, oblivious to the tension that had been building. Brown pounced on him.

> "Here! Why did n't you tell me we'd got to land at that plantation?"
>
> "I did tell you, Mr. Brown."
>
> "It's a lie!"
>
> I said:—
>
> "You lie yourself. He did tell you."[23]

This outburst of Sam's—his second direct challenge of Brown—unhinged the pilot. He stared at Sam, then turned to Henry and ordered him out of the pilothouse. Mark Twain recalled that as the boy started to leave, Brown snatched a heavy lump of coal and made as if to hit him with it; "but I was between, with a heavy stool, and I hit Brown a good honest blow which stretched him out."[24] Then Sam fell upon his tormentor and pounded him with his fists—the only act of physical violence for which Samuel Clemens was ever known. The struggle on the floor lasted perhaps five minutes. A crowd gathered on the hurricane deck to watch it. While all this was happening, the 486-ton *Pennsylvania* wafted along in the current, fifteen miles an hour, with no one at the wheel to control its rudders.

William Brown eventually struggled out from beneath the pummeling Sam and grabbed the wheel. Luckily, the steamboat was drifting down the middle of a deep channel in a full river. After he had stabilized the boat, Brown raged at Sam to leave the pilothouse, brandishing a spyglass. Sam elected to stay awhile, mocking the man he had just humiliated. This moment irresistibly calls Charlie Chaplin to mind; the Tramp, having gained the edge over some bullying authority-figure, sticking around to rub it in a little before hotfooting it to safety. ("I tarried, and criticised [sic] his grammar; I reformed his ferocious speeches for him, and put them into good English, calling his attention to the advantage of pure English over the bastard dialect of the Pennsylvanian collieries whence he was extracted . . . "[25])

Captain Klinefelter was waiting for him beside the door. He led Sam into a small parlor and grilled him about the brawl. Mark Twain recalled that after he had confessed to flattening Brown and then pummeling him ("I supposed I was booked for the penitentiary sure"), the captain surprised him by announcing his sympathy for the attack.

> I'm deuced glad of it! Hark ye, never mention that I said that. You have been guilty of a great crime; and don't you ever be guilty of it again, on this boat. *But*—lay for him ashore! Give him a good sound thrashing, do you hear? I 'll pay the expenses. Now go—[26]

In the end it was Sam and Henry who paid the expenses. With the inevitability of Greek drama, the consequences of Sam's fight with William Brown—and of Sam's two outbursts of truth-telling on Henry's behalf, which guaranteed the confrontation—began to spread themselves through the brothers' destinies, like pent-up water rushing through a sluice-gate that has been opened.

Brown, coming off his watch, confronted Klinefelter and demanded that "*one* of us—either himself or Sam—be put ashore immediately. (Obviously, he assumed that Sam would be the one removed from the boat.) "Very well," Klinefelter replied, "Let it be yourself."[27] His bluff called, Brown stalked back to the pilothouse. If any faint hope had existed for repairing the standoff between himself and Sam, none existed now.

In New Orleans, Klinefelter searched for a pilot to replace Brown on the return voyage upriver. After three days he had not succeeded. Brown made it clear that he would not set foot aboard a boat that included Sam Clemens. The *Pennsylvania*'s captain offered another solution: He would arrange passage to St. Louis for Sam aboard another boat, the *A. T. Lacey.* Once in St. Louis, Klinefelter would replace Brown and restore Sam to his position as steersman. Henry, unobtrusive as always, would remain on board the *Pennsylvania.* All concerned parties agreed.

The last night that Sam and Henry were to spend together was a languorous evening of intimate conversation on a freight pile on the riverfront in ripe New Orleans. Whatever passed between them on that night became enfolded, along with the Laura Wright encounter and the dream of Henry in the metallic burial case, into the operatic remembrance that Mark Twain reconstructed, episodically, over the remainder of his life, most conspicuously in *Life on the Mississippi* and in his autobiographical dictations. Like other elements in this intensely braided and textured libretto of the early river summer of 1858, the objective truth of it can never be fully known. Twain himself never conjoined all the remarkable, highly suggestive subplots of those fateful weeks into a unified narrative; the elements of his foredoomed romance with Laura and of his struggle with Brown, as sub-verses in the great threnody for his brother, remain sequestered in two separate texts, their resonating metaphors never integrated by him into the whole.

As to that final evening together on the freight pile:

> The subject of the chat, mainly, was one which I think we had not exploited before—steamboat disasters. One was then on its way to us, little as we suspected it; the water which was to make the steam which should cause it, was washing past some point fifteen hundred miles up the river while we talked;—but it would arrive at the right time and the right place . . . we decided that if a disaster ever fell within our experience we would at least stick to the boat, and give such minor service as chance might throw in the

> way. Henry remembered this, afterward, when the disaster came, and acted accordingly.[28]

Henry left New Orleans on the *Pennsylvania* the next morning. The *A.T. Lacey* pulled out two days later, on June 11, with Sam aboard. Among its pilots was Barton Bowen, Will's brother.

It was at Greenville, Mississippi, two days afterward, that Sam received the first intimation of tragedy. A stranger on the levee was shouting: "The *Pennsylvania* is blown up at Ship Island, and a hundred fifty lives lost!"[29] The date was June 13, Henry Clemens's twentieth birthday.

At Napoleon, Arkansas, the *Lacey* crew found copies of a Memphis newspaper, an "extra" edition that reported some details. Henry Clemens's name was listed; he was described as unhurt.

Farther along, another extra surfaced. This one reported, as Mark Twain recalled, that Henry was "hurt beyond help."[30]

The *Lacey* steamed on, upriver. Within a hundred miles of Memphis its crew began to see more direct evidence of catastrophe: debris from the *Pennsylvania*'s superstructure, and human corpses carried along in the current.

The explosion had occurred about four miles upriver from Ship Island, some seventy miles below Memphis, at around 6 a.m. on Sunday the thirteenth. Apparently the *Pennsylvania* had engaged in a race with a rival steamboat, and had just taken on a load of wood for fuel-burning in preparation for another race: The firemen on board were tossing pine-knots and coal into the furnace—despite knowledge that at least one of the ship's boilers suffered a bad leak.

Four boilers went up in the initial outburst, splintering the forward third of the boat, including the pilothouse. The sudden nebula of steam killed the firemen and many of the passengers on deck. No one who breathed the scalding vapor survived. Most of the deaths* occurred in this opening instant. The pilot William Brown went flying into the Mississippi on a trajectory of steam. He was seized by a coal-boat pilot named Reed Young, who had hold of a life preserver, but he died in Young's arms, muttering, "My poor wife and children."[31]

Captain Klinefelter was sitting in a barber's chair when the boilers blew, waiting for a shave. He was unhurt, but the released energy tore a gigantic hole in the floor directly behind his chair; in front of it the barber stood for several seconds after the impact, "still stirring his lather unconsciously, and saying not a word."[32] A priest was impaled with a crowbar and died horribly. The fifteen-year-old son of a French admiral, wrote Twain, "was fearfully scalded, but bore his tortures manfully."[33]

Many people were killed, hurt, or trapped by the debris launched into the air by the explosion as it fell back on the boat. Another pilot, a gentle Shakespeare-reading friend of Sam's named George Ealer, escaped serious injury when the boat's heavy pilot-wheel landed near him. In shock, Ealer collected the pieces to his chess set and the joints of his flute before disembarking the stricken boat.

Henry Clemens had been sleeping in a stateroom directly above the boilers. Like Brown, he was propelled into the river by the blast. Unlike Brown, he did not die right away.

---

*No one knows how many people were killed in this explosion; the loss of the ship's register and the many immigrants traveling on "deck passage" have made a precise tabulation impossible. Mark Twain himself, perhaps going on the early newspaper estimates, reported three hundred lives lost. Captain Klinefelter put the number at thirty-eight. Other estimates ranged between twenty and one hundred-sixty. The editors of *Mark Twain's Letters, Vol. 1,* have suggested that "eighty to one hundred deaths seems a reasonable estimate," although they acknowledge that the total could have been much higher.

Exactly what happened to Henry, and to the *Pennsylvania,* after those first concussive moments are matters of confusion, conflicting testimony, and, perhaps, Mark Twain's compulsive search for meaning within patterns, howsoever those patterns needed to be invented. The onset of the fire, for instance: Twain wrote that fire broke out on what remained of the boat "after a little." At least one other contemporary report had the conflagration starting within a minute after the boilers exploded. But George C. Harrison, the son of the owner of the woodyard landing where the steamboat had just taken on fuel, told a newspaper that the fire did not take hold "for some thirty or forty minutes (perhaps longer) after the explosion,"[34] which allowed the Harrisons and others time to evacuate a number of passengers and crew—nearly two hundred onto the Harrison wood-boat alone.

Everyone agreed, though, that when the fire began, it spread—in Harrison's words—"with the greatest rapidity."[35] Soon the superstructure was a burning mass, intensely heated. Twain wrote of a "striker" unhurt but imprisoned in the debris: "when he saw that the fire was likely to drive away the workers, he begged that some one would shoot him, and thus save him from the more dreadful death . . . [rescuers] had to listen to this poor fellow's supplications till the flames ended his miseries."[36] The image of the Tramp imprisoned in the burning Hannibal jail could not have been far from Twain's mind as he wrote these lines.

Then there was the uncertain matter of Henry's fate once he hit the water. In a letter written from Memphis, Sam told his relatives, somewhat ambiguously, that Henry had first fallen back on the hot boilers, then was bombarded by falling rubbish, and that finally he "got into the water and swam to shore, and got into the flatboat with the other survivors."[37] (Why Henry would have climbed into the flatboat after reaching shore was not explained.) In a tribute to Henry published a few weeks after the disaster, Sam repeated the image of Henry falling back on the boilers, then "extricating himself" and escaping on a mattress or raft to an open rescue boat, "where he lay exposed . . . to the wind and the scorching rays of a Southern sun, for eight hours . . ."[38]

By the time of *Life on the Mississippi,* written mostly in 1882, Mark Twain had finally distilled his version, or vision, of Henry's fate:

> When Mr. Wood [another clerk] and Henry fell in the water, they struck out for shore, which was only a few hundred yards away; but Henry presently said he believed he was unhurt (what an unaccountable error!) and therefore would swim back to the boat and help save the wounded. So they parted, and Henry returned.

Thus Twain consummated, in his art, the conversation Henry and Sam had had on the freight pile in New Orleans the night before the *Pennsylvania* disembarked.

Whatever his actions, Henry was eventually loaded with other survivors onto the steamer *Kate Frisbee* and transported the sixty miles to Memphis. There, nearly a full day after the explosion, they were placed on mattresses in a vast makeshift hospital inside the Memphis Exchange and attended by volunteer doctors and nurses. This is how Sam found Henry when he arrived at Memphis on Tuesday, June 15. After viewing his brother, Sam sent a terse telegraph—in which his last name was misspelled—to the Moffett household in St. Louis:

> Henrys recovery is very doubtful [signed] Sam Clements[39]

A local newspaper reporter was present when Sam rushed into the Memphis Exchange. His account of Sam's reaction told of the depths of agony beneath that terse information:

> We witnessed one of the most affecting scenes at the Exchange yesterday that has ever been seen. The brother of Mr. Henry Clemens, second clerk of the *Pennsylvania*, who now lies dangerously ill from the injuries received by the explosion of that boat, arrived in the city yesterday afternoon, on the steamer *A. T. Lacy* [sic]. He hurried to the Exchange to see his brother, and on approaching the bedside of the wounded man, his feelings so much overcame him, at the scalded and emaciated form before him, that he sunk to the floor overpowered. There was scarcely a dry eye in the house; the poor sufferers shed tears at the sight. This brother had been pilot on the *Pennsylvania*, but fortunately for him, had remained in New Orleans when the boat started up.[40]

That phrase, "fortunately for him," and its variants would enflame Sam Clemens/Mark Twain's torture in the years to come. Beginning while he was still watching over his brother, and continuing upon his return to the river several weeks later, Sam found himself festooned with a new nickname in honor of his evasion of the catastrophe: "Lucky."

Lucky? Lucky that he would have to live on with the memory of coaxing his younger brother out of his libraries and onto the *Pennsylvania?* Lucky to live with the twisted consequences of his fight with Brown—his own saving removal from the doomed boat while Henry, whom he'd sought to save, churned upriver to his oblivion? No, Sam was not lucky. Sam was responsible. He was as responsible for Henry's death as he had been for the death of his brother Ben in his enigmatic "treachery" to him; as responsible as he had been for the drownings of Dutchy and "Lem Hackett" as revealed in the prophetic lightning over Hannibal; as responsible as he had been for the incineration of the tramp. Among all the American national tendencies that Mark Twain embodied, or became enmeshed in, perhaps none was more gothically emblematic than this one: the tendency to run afoul of the law of unintended consequences, to see one's innocent magnanimous impulses converted bewilderingly to flaming devastation.

No, "luck" was not the point of his survival. The point was culpability, the annealing of his guilty conscience and the beginning of a lifelong flight from incarceration inside his damned human self.

Luck? Luck—or envy—was the privilege of the dead, as he pointed out in a torrent of dark aphorisms late in his life. "Whoever has lived long enough to find out what life is, knows how deep a debt of gratitude we owe to Adam, the first benefactor of our race. He brought death into the world," Mark Twain would write, and: "Why is it that we rejoice at a birth and grieve at a funeral? It is because we are not involved," and: "All say, 'How hard it is that we have to die'—a strange complaint to come from the mouths of people who have had to live."[41]

He unleashed a strong foretaste of this anguished self-recrimination in a letter from Memphis to Mollie Clemens on Friday, June 18, while Henry still lay critically ill:

> *Long before this reaches you, my poor Henry,—my darling, my pride, my glory, my* all, *will have finished his blameless career, and the light of my life will have gone out in utter darkness.*

> *O, God! This is hard to bear. Hardened, hopeless,—aye, lost—lost—lost and ruined sinner as I am—I, even* I, *have humbled myself to the ground and prayed as never man prayed before, that the great God might let this cup pass from me—that he would strike me to the earth, but spare my brother—that he would pour out the fulness [sic] of his just wrath upon my wicked head, but have mercy, mercy, mercy upon that unoffending boy . . . poor wretched me, that was once so proud, was humbled to the very dust—lower than dust—for the vilest beggar in the streets of St. Louis could never conceive a humiliation like mine. Men take me by the hand and* congratulate *me, and call me* **"lucky"** *because I was not on the Pennsylvania when she blew up! May God forgive them, for they know not what they say!*[42]

Henry died at about dawn on June 21. Sam, nearly out of his mind with grief, rested a few hours at a private home, then accompanied his brother's body to St. Louis via steamer. A young man from Memphis went along to look after Sam. Orion hurried home from Jamestown, Tennessee. Jane Clemens and the Moffetts joined the cortege that bore the body to Hannibal, where he was buried on June 25 in the Baptist cemetery on the top of the hill, next to John Marshall. In 1876 both bodies were transferred to the new Mount Olivet cemetery south of town, above the river.

In his old age, Mark Twain recalled (or, more probably, invented) yet another layer of pathos surrounding the loss, another reason for self-flagellation and guilt. Henry had not died from his scalding wounds, but from a misdosage of medication; and the bumbler who commanded that misdosage was Sam Clemens. The sequence, in Twain's mind, was as follows: A Memphis doctor named Thomas F. Peyton had paid special attention to Henry through the week of his suffering. Though Sam's letters at the time mention nothing of it, his reverie convinced him that Dr. Peyton, "a fine and large-hearted old physician of great reputation in the community," had succeeded in bringing Henry out of danger. Peyton then suggested that, in order to assure Henry's peaceful sleep, Sam ask the physician on watch to administer an eighth of a grain of morphine to the boy. The physicians, "young fellows hardly out of college," botched the dosage, giving Henry "a vast quantity heaped on a knife-blade." This proved to be the fatal stroke. If only Sam had not insisted on that morphine . . . [43]

There was the final matter of the consummation of the dream.

While Sam slept off his fatigue in the private home (as he recalled it in his memoirs) something was happening at the Memphis Exchange. Most of the dead victims had been placed in unpainted coffins of white pine, but Henry had been a favorite with the women volunteers, and they had made up a fund of sixty dollars and bought a metallic case. When Sam returned to the Exchange and saw Henry, he recognized his dream, reproduced. Henry was even wearing Sam's clothes.

> And I think I missed one detail; but that one was immediately supplied, for just then an elderly lady entered the place with a large bouquet consisting mainly of white roses, and in the centre of it was a red rose, and she laid it on his breast.[44]

Sam Clemens's youth ended with the consummation of that dream. His boyhood was buried in the coffin with Henry. Nothing of his correspondence survived the ensuing nine months. He returned to the river about a month after the funeral and remained on it until the Civil War interrupted steamboat traffic there. He piloted with various of the Bowen brothers; haunted New Orleans and immersed himself in Mardi Gras; applied for membership in the Masons and was accepted; saw a fortuneteller regarding Laura Wright. He departed the riverlife in St. Louis in May 1861, stepping off the *Nebraska*, the last boat to enjoy free passage upriver through the Union blockade at Memphis. He hid out at the Moffett home, fearing arrest by Union agents; joined the Confederate volunteer group, the Marion Rangers, in mid-June; lasted two weeks; then lit out west with Orion, who had been appointed secretary of the Nevada Territory in a document signed by Abraham Lincoln. There he prospected for silver and gold, found none, set a mountain on fire, drank heavily, never spoke of the War nor of Henry, took up with a proto-countercultural enclave of wild and gifted journalists in Virginia City, and became the central figure in their improvisation of a surreal, fabricating, fabulating new form of newspapering that received attention and reproduction back East.

In the Territory, on February 3, 1863, a month after Lincoln announced the Emancipation Proclamation, Sam Clemens found emancipation from his own enslavement of the soul. At age twenty-eight he discovered and entered into his immortal pseudonym, Mark Twain. Something in this name released him from himself; the alias took the function of a magical mask, or a gorgeous puppet, through which he could address the world in voices not identifiably his own. As "Mark Twain," he would invent a new literature borne on the currents of dialect, but in its deepest fathoms concerned with a kind of resurrection: the resurrection of humor from the abyss of pathos, hostility, tragedy, and loss. Sweet Henry, so silent in life, would speak forever through his brother's pen. Among Mark Twain's most recurrent themes would be twinning—the diverging but inextricable fates of brothers; the perverse fortunes of switched identity; the unstable boundaries between dream and reality; the dialectic between innocence and fallen man. The first sentence of the first essay he published under his new pen name read: "I feel very much as if I had just awakened out of a long sleep." He had indeed awakened, emerged as from a dream into his genius. In "Mark Twain" he had found his frame; in his lifelong flight from the melancholy of Henry's flowered metal casket, and from his childhood, and from the nighttime terrors of Hannibal's embrace, he had become his own tall tale.

Seventeen

"I . . . bid you farewell."

On May 29, 1902, a year and a half after his return to America, Mark Twain reentered the long dark dream of his boyhood and visited Hannibal for the last time.

He was sixty-six. At the height of his public celebrity, he was likewise at the height of his private ruminations on the pain of existence. He had been working on the baleful "Extracts from Adam's Diary" and "The Death Disk"; the outlines of "The Mysterious Stranger" had entered his fantasies; "Amended Obituaries" and "Was It Heaven? Or Hell?" would see print before the year's end.

On this last week of May 1902, Mark Twain was ascendant as few men in history, and no literary figure, had ever been ascendant. He was a known figure throughout the world. Before the gaze of the nations, he had circled the globe and raised a fortune with his lectures to pay his creditors and erase his stupendous bankruptcy. He had been translated into all the important languages. He had met Freud in Vienna and had a private audience with the Austrian emperor Franz-Joseph. He had been compared to Cervantes, Shakespeare. Prestigious Howells had called him "sole, incomparable . . . the Lincoln of our literature." Oxford waited to drape him in its robes. People wanted his autograph. The dukes and dauphins of the world made risky fortunes claiming his identity.

In his native land, which he had mythified for a previously skeptical world, it had been even more intense. He had become the first public man to cause frenzy on the streets, to trigger the release of an American obsession that, once released, would renew its energies again and again, like a rage against the absence of the numinous in a democracy. This was the obsessive need to worship a secular god.

His world and his new century were still sunlit. Marchese Marconi was working toward the transmission of the first transatlantic radio signal. The Wright Brothers were working toward liftoff at Kitty Hawk. Halley's Comet was hurtling toward the solar neighborhood. The first World Series was a little more than a year away.

He had been invited to receive an honorary degree from the University of Missouri at Columbia on June 4. Still, his preliminary detour to Hannibal was unannounced; he wrote to no one there in advance of his coming.

In 1902 Hannibal was a far more ambitious burg than the white town drowsing in the sunshine of a summer's morning that Sam Clemens had languished through in the 1840s. It was a railroad center—John Marshall's dream, consummated—and stout red brick had replaced most of the white clapboard. Its population had reached 12,500 and was climbing. It was a city of merchants and manufacturers; cement; shoes; the Bluff City (a boosterish salute to the embrasure of hills). A city quite proud, thank you, to trumpet Mark Twain as its foremost native son. Perhaps that is why he did not communicate in advance.

He slipped into town on a late-afternoon weekday train from St. Louis, accompanied by an awed book reviewer from the *Post-Dispatch* named Robertus Love. The newspaper had given Love the assignment of following Twain around Hannibal and writing up the "color" of the visit; and Love filed dispatches reporting virtually his every movement and inflating every nuance.

> Hannibal had no idea that Mark Twain was coming when he did. . . . "If we had known he was aboard that train," remarked a citizen, "the Union Depot platform would not have been big enough to hold the chairmen of committees."[1]

Twain walked the single block from the train station to the Windsor Hotel,* where he had booked a room. Love trailed along, alert for comic byplay, which the great man indulgently provided:

Will Sutton, the hotel clerk, remarked:

> "Mr. Clemens, I was born close to your birthplace at Florida, and have been in the house where you were born, often."
>
> "I was not born often—only once," responded the humorist; "but I'm glad to see you, all the same."[2]

The next morning he presented himself before the house at 206 Hill Street and certified its landmark status by proclaiming it his boyhood residence. He posed for a photographer in its front door in a

*The Windsor stood at 125 South Main, just a block from where the Mark Twain Hotel would rise three years later. It lasted until 1962, when it was torn down for a parking lot.

light gray suit, hands thrust into his jacket-pockets; the resulting image would continue to be reproduced on postcards throughout the century. Then he entered a carriage in the company of a wealthy widow named Helen Garth and was driven to Mt. Olivet Cemetery overlooking the Mississippi, where he viewed the gravesites of Jane, who had died in 1890, and John Marshall, and Orion, and Henry.

"It is very beautifully situated, that cemetery," he told Robertus Love upon returning to the hotel. "If I had the time I should look for the boys out there." He meant the boys of his youth. "That is where they are . . . most of them are out there in that cemetery. I could pick them out if I had the time to walk about and read their names."[3]

By this time an entourage had gathered. Old men crowded into the hotel office to announce their names to him and make their claims of boyhood friendship. Some of these, he recognized.

> "How are you doing, Eddie?" he inquired of Mr. Pierce.
>
> "Like yourself, Sam," replied the schoolmate, "like a cow's tail going down."[4]

A mob was waiting for him at the Farmers and Merchants Bank, where a reception had been arranged. More old chums pled for recognition.

> "Hello, Sam," said one old man; "I'm Lippincott, and used to play marbles with you, but probably you remember my brother, Dave Lippincott." Mr. Clemens could not recall the Lippincotts.
>
> "You and Dave and I and Charley Buchanan used to—"
>
> "Ah, Charley Buchanan," said the humorist. "Yes, indeed. I remember Charley."[5]

He told everyone he would make a speech if he could think of a topic. And then he went off to a ceremony at Jane's old Presbyterian church. That evening he distributed some diplomas to the Hannibal High School graduating class of 1902.

The town had quickly worked itself into a frenzy over his presence. By Friday afternoon the populace had begun to costume itself in his honor—as it would continue to do episodically for the next hundred years. Robertus Love took it all in.

> Today Hannibal is full of Huck Finns, Tom Sawyers and Beckys.
>
> There are more "originals" of Huck, Tom and Becky in this town since Mark Twain arrived than one would expect to meet in a staid old town with 23 respectable Sunday schools and a Salvation Army.
>
> You don't need to bait your hook if you go fishing for a Huck. Just make a cast anywhere around town, and there's your Huckleberry.

Love encountered the obligatory citizen who didn't get it.

> "I've lived in this town 71 years," remarked one reputable native, "and forever was accused of being Huck Finn until last night. I submit that my reputation has been good, and if I ever was Huckleberry Finn, I can't recall it. It's a base slander to put upon a man in his old age."[6]

On Friday evening, Hannibal's jamboree of costumery and role-playing in its native son's honor reached a surreal apogee. In a staged encounter of multiple identities, the kind of stroke that would have sealed a publicist's career nine or ten decades in the future, Mark Twain/Samuel Clemens/Tom Sawyer sat down to dinner with Laura Frazier/Laura Hawkins/Becky Thatcher.

In describing the event, the *Post-Dispatch* reporter fell into a moist swoon of rhetoric—of "showing off."

> Sam Clemens and Laura Hawkins, both aged 15, ate dinner together Friday evening. They were guests of Mrs. Helen Garth, at her costly mansion on South Fifth Street.
>
> Sam, who in the future is destined to be one Mark Twain, genial humorist and one of the most famous men in the world, and Laura Hawkins, whose star of fortune reads that she will become the Widow Frazier and serve as matron for the Home of the Friendless in Hannibal—these two, playmates in 1840, schoolmates in 1845, and pledged sweethearts in this present year of 1850—met Friday evening at dinner, with Mrs. Garth as chaperone.
>
> Strange to say, Sam was staying at the Windsor Hotel on Main street instead of at his mother's house on Hill street. This Hannibal boy of 15 was reveling in the splendors of two connecting rooms, with a whole bed to himself and also a wardrobe for his clothes.
>
> Just why he left home the Hannibal people—the whole 700 of them—are not quite sure, but it is hinted at Brittingham's drug store, around the corner from the Widow Clemens' house, that Sam has found at last a large quantity of the buried treasure in Loop Hollow, north of Holliday's hill, and is enjoying the luxuries . . . [7]

. . . And so on. Twain, ever the trouper, entered the spirit of the moment, played out the role. Upon his first glimpse of his former playmate, he cried out, "Gee whiz—it seems like I ain't seen you in 50 years, Laura."

Later, Twain received a delegation from the high school graduating class in the parlors of the Windsor Hotel; they presented him with a souvenir spoon that bore an engraving of the house on Hill Street. As he looked at the image of the house on the spoon, Twain was moved for some reason to remember his boyhood attempt to contract measles from Will Bowen. He recounted for the young people, who were conceivably unprepared for such a story, how he had jumped from the upper window of his bedroom into a pile of sand, and from there had run to the infected Bowen house.

"I was very near to death," he told the group, "and I have never had such a good opportunity to die. Sometimes I think I should have embraced the opportunity, thereby escaping many unpleasant things. But I have survived to enjoy some pleasant things, and this occasion is one of them. So it is worth while that I was cured of the measles."[8]

That flash of morbidity was but a prelude that foreshadowed a seizure of lamentation during a speech on the following night, his last ever in the town. The past spilled down upon him and he gave out a cry of anguish that shocked Robertus Love, shocked the five hundred men and women in attendance before him, shocked Laura Frazier who had come to watch and listen; shocked himself, probably: the shock of a man confronted with ghosts. Or rather, the shock of a man confronted with a recessional of ghosts: the ghosts of Margaret and Benjamin and John Marshall and Henry and Jane and Suzy and Orion; the ghosts of all the boys up in the graveyard; the ghost of his own boyhood self. All exiting the stage before his eyes.

His cry was of a man either emerging from or sinking helplessly into a dream.

The occasion was a speech at a women's charitable group called the Labinnah Club—Labinnah being "Hannibal" spelled backwards. Until the moment of his anguished cry, Mark Twain had been stunning, debonair, at the top of his form. "A moment before," wrote Love, "the scores of beautiful girls and matrons, handsomely gowned, and the clubmen and their friends had been laughing heartily at the flashes of Mark Twain's characteristic wit." He had been introduced to the gathering by a local minister, "in flattering terms," and quipped in response that it was hard to reply to such an introduction because all the good things said of him were true. He said some other funny things. He said something that had everyone helpless with mirth.

"His audience roared," Love wrote. "It was said so humorously that laughter exploded like a volcano. Everybody was saying to himself: 'He is the funniest man on earth.'"

Then came the stunning moment. Twain abruptly bowed his head, and his shoulders shook. Love thought that he appeared to be groping for words. "He mumbled something that was not understood, and at last he looked up into the now tense, sympathetic faces of his auditors."

And then Mark Twain became Sam Clemens once again.

"I realize that this must be my last visit to Hannibal," he said to the people who were looking at him, "and in bidding you hail I also bid you farewell."

> His voice was choked, his utterance was broken. It was the almost wailing voice of an old man who realized that the

> years are behind him and that he is bidding farewell forever and ever to the haunts and comrades of his childhood days, leaving home never to return.
>
> Mark Twain apparently had forgotten all save his early life and the consciousness of increasing age. He had forgotten his world-wide fame, the plaudits of princes, the friendship of emperors, the adulation of the multitudes of many lands.
>
> He had forgotten his books and his splendid home in the East.
>
> Nothing remained to him save the past of half a century ago and the insistent clamor of that inward voice crying across the years: "Farewell, farewell."

By the next day—Sunday, the first of June, departure day—he had recovered his aplomb and his sense of humor. He asked a Baptist minister, the Rev. Everett Gill, to walk across town with him to his hotel, where his luggage awaited him. "It will give me a better standing in Hannibal," he pronounced, "to be seen on the street with a preacher."

At the railroad station, waiting for his connection to Columbia, he stood with a spray of flowers in his fist and posed for photographers one more time. Deaf Tom Nash, wraithlike, stepped from the crowd then, and called out, "Same damned fools, Sam!"

And then, as it had been on the June day of forty-nine years ago, it was time to go. A train took him away from his youth this time, instead of a river packet. In leaving Hannibal for the last time, he was saying farewell to the ghost of a national past, of an American Arcadia, of an American concept of "the past," a concept he had largely created and placed in his boyhood books for preservation. Evaporating now, that ghost, in the substantial glare of electricity, in the metal hum of the telephone, in Marconi's waves and Einstein's curvatures, and in the gathering thunder of munitions the likes of which the Connecticut Yankee himself could not have imagined.

Times had changed, and water was giving way to fire.

SELECTED BIBLIOGRAPHY

Books

Blair, Walter, *Mark Twain's Hannibal, Huck & Tom,* Berkeley: University of California Press, 1969.

Bloom, Harold, ed., *Mark Twain: Modern Critical Views,* New York: Chelsea House, 1986.

Bridgman, Edgar M., *Traveling in Mark Twain,* Berkeley: University of California Press, 1987.

Brooks, Van Wyck, *The Ordeal of Mark Twain,* New York: Dutton, 1920.

Cox, James M., *Mark Twain: The Fate of Humor,* Princeton, N.J.: Princeton University Press, 1966.

DeVoto, Bernard, *Mark Twain's America,* Boston: Little, Brown, 1932.

______, *Mark Twain at Work,* Cambridge, Mass.: Harvard University Press, 1942.

Dunlop, M. H., *Sixty Miles from Contentment,* New York: Basic Books, 1995.

Emerson, Everett, *The Authentic Mark Twain,* Philadelphia: University of Pennsylvania Press, 1984.

Fatout, Paul, *Mark Twain in Virginia City,* Bloomington: Indiana University Press, 1960.

Ferguson, DeLancy, *Mark Twain: Man and Legend,* New York: Charter Books, 1963.

Fishkin, Shelly Fisher, *Lighting Out for the Territory: Reflections on Mark Twain and American Culture,* New York: Oxford University Press, 1997.

Gribben, Alan, *Mark Twain's Library: A Reconstruction,* Boston: G. K. Hall, 1980.

Hagood, J. Hurley and Roberta, *The Story of Hannibal: A Bicentennial History, 1976,* Hannibal: The Hannibal Free Public Library/Standard Printing Co., 1976.

Hecht, Ben, *A Child of the Century,* New York: Primus/Donald I. Fine, 1985.

Holcombe, R. I., *History of Marion County Missouri 1884,* reprinted for the Marion County Historical Society, Marceline, Mo.: Walsworth, 1979.

Howells, William Dean, *My Mark Twain: Reminiscences and Criticisms,* New York: Harper & Bros., 1910.

Hunter, Louis C., *Steamboats on the Western Rivers,* Boston: Harvard University Press, 1949.

Kaplan, Justin, *Mark Twain and His World: America's Greatest Writer and Wit,* New York: Crescent Books, 1974.

______, *Mr. Clemens and Mark Twain: A Biography,* New York: Simon & Schuster, 1966.

Kerouac, Jack, *On the Road* (40th Anniversary Edition), New York: Viking, 1997.

Kruse, Horst, *Mark Twain and Life on the Mississippi,* Boston: University of Massachusetts Press, 1981.

Lauber, John, *The Making of Mark Twain,* New York: American Heritage, 1985.

Lewisohn, Ludwig, *Expression in America,* New York: Harper & Bros., 1932.

Lynn, Kenneth, *Mark Twain and Southwestern Humor,* Boston: Atlantic Monthly Press, 1959.

Macnaughton, William R., *Mark Twain's Last Years as a Writer,* Columbia: University of Missouri Press, 1979.

Mark Twain–Howells Letters, edited by William M. Gibson and Henry Nash Smith, Cambridge, Mass.: Harvard University Press, 1960.

Mark Twain: Tales, Speeches, Essays, and Sketches, edited by Tom Quirk, New York: Penguin Classics, 1994.

Mark Twain's Letters, Volume 1: 1853–1866, edited by Edgar Marquess Branch, Michael B. Frank, and Kenneth M. Sanderson, Berkeley: University of California Press, 1988.

Mark Twain's Notebooks and Journals, Volume 1: 1855–1873, edited by Frederick Anderson, Michael B. Frank, and Kenneth M. Sanderson, *The Mark Twain Papers,* Berkeley: University of California Press, 1975.

Mark Twain's Satires and Burlesques, edited by Franklin R. Rogers, Berkeley: University of California Press, 1967.

Michelson, Bruce, *Mark Twain on the Loose: A Comic Writer and the American Self,* Amherst: University of Massachusetts Press, 1995.

Paine, Albert Bigelow, *The Adventures of Mark Twain,* New York: Grosset & Dunlap, 1915.

______, *Mark Twain: A Biography: The Personal and Literary Life of Samuel Langhorne Clemens,* New York: Harper & Bros., 1912.

Parini, Jay, *John Steinbeck: A Biography,* New York: Holt, 1995.

Perelman, S. J., *The Road to Milltown, or Under the Spreading Atrophy,* New York: Simon & Schuster, 1957.

Rasmussen, R. Kent, *Mark Twain A to Z: The Essential Reference to His Life and Writings,* New York: Facts on File, 1995.

Sanborn, Margaret, *Mark Twain: The Bachelor Years,* New York: Doubleday, 1990.

Schudson, Michael, *Discovering the News,* New York: Basic Books, 1978.

Tocqueville, Alexis de, *Democracy in America,* New York: Harper & Row, 1966.

Twain, Mark, *The Adventures of Huckleberry Finn: The Only Comprehensive Edition,* Foreword and Addendum by Victor Doyno, New York: Random House, 1996.

______, *The Adventures of Tom Sawyer,* New York: Oxford University Press, 1996.

______, *The Autobiography of Mark Twain,* edited by Charles Neider, New York: Harper & Row, 1959.

______, *The Celebrated Jumping Frog of Calaveras County, and Other Sketches,* edited by Shelly Fisher Fishkin, New York and Oxford: Oxford University Press, 1996.

______, *The Complete Humorous Sketches* and *Tales of Mark Twain,* Garden City, N.Y.: Hanover House, 1961.

______, *A Connecticut Yankee in King Arthur's Court,* New York: Oxford University Press, 1996.

______, *Following the Equator* and *Anti-Imperialist Essays*, New York: Oxford University Press, 1996.

______, *The Innocents Abroad,* New York: Oxford University Press, 1996.

______, *Letters from the Earth,* edited by Bernard DeVoto, New York: Perennial Library, 1974.

______, *Life on the Mississippi,* New York: Oxford University Press, 1996.

______, *Pudd'nhead Wilson,* New York: Penguin Classics, 1986.

______, *Roughing It,* New York: Oxford University Press, 1996.

______, *The Works of Mark Twain: Early Tales and Sketches, Volume 1, 1851–1864,* edited by Edgar Marquess Branch and Robert H. Hirst, with the assistance of Harriet Elinor Smith, Berkeley: University of California Press, 1979.

______, and Charles Dudley Warner, *The Gilded Age: A Tale of Today*, New York: Meridian, 1994.

Wecter, Dixon, *Sam Clemens of Hannibal,* Boston: Houghton Mifflin, 1952.

Whitman, Walt, *Leaves of Grass,* New York: Penguin Books, 1975.

Wonham, Henry B., *Mark Twain and the Art of the Tall Tale,* New York: Oxford University Press, 1993.

Periodicals

The Hannibal *Courier-Post,* April 21, 1910.

The *New York Times,* October 16, 1900.

The *North American Review,* March and April 1907.

The St. Louis *Post-Dispatch,* May 30, 1902.

NOTES

Chapter 1

1. Cited by Justin Kaplan, *Mr. Clemens and Mark Twain: A Biography* (New York: Simon & Schuster, 1966).

2. Twain's dockside comments are quoted from the October 16, 1900, edition of the *New York Times.*

3. Ibid.

4. "Chapters from My Autobiography," *The North American Review* (April 5, 1907); dictated October 1906.

5. Kaplan, op. cit.

6. From the clippings file of the Mark Twain Papers, Bancroft Library, the University of California, Berkeley; quoted by William R. Macnaughton in *Mark Twain's Last Years as a Writer* (Columbia: University of Missouri Press, 1979).

7. Quoted in *The Autobiography of Mark Twain,* edited by Charles Neider (New York: Harper & Row, 1959).

8. Ibid.

9. 1910 essay reprinted in G. K. Chesterton, *A Handful of Authors: Essays on Books and Writers,* edited by Dorothy Collins (New York: Sheed & Ward, 1953).

10. William Dean Howells, *My Mark Twain: Reminiscences and Criticisms* (New York: Harper & Bros., 1910).

11. *Mark Twain–Howells Letters,* edited by William M. Gibson and Henry Nash Smith (Cambridge, Mass.: Harvard University Press, 1960); quoted by Macnaughton.

12. *Letters from the Earth,* edited by Bernard DeVoto (New York: Perennial Library, 1974).

13. Justin Kaplan, *Mark Twain and His World: America's Greatest Writer and Wit* (New York: Crescent Books, 1974).

14. *Mark Twain–Howells Letters,* quoted by Kaplan, *Mr. Clemens and Mark Twain.*

15. *Mark Twain–Howells Letters,* quoted by Macnaughton, op. cit.

16. Mark Twain's notebooks.

Chapter 2

1. Alexis de Tocqueville, *Democracy in America,* part I, ch. 3 (New York: Harper & Row, 1966).

2. Ibid.

3. Dixon Wecter, *Sam Clemens of Hannibal* (Boston: Houghton Mifflin, 1952).

4. Quoted by Walter Blair, op. cit. Walter Blair, *Mark Twain's Hannibal, Huck & Tom*, Berkeley: University of California Press, 1969.

5. Ibid.

6. Ibid.

7. Ibid.

8. Ibid.

9. *The Adventures of Tom Sawyer* (New York: Oxford University Press, 1996).

10. *Pudd'nhead Wilson* (New York: Penguin Classics, 1986).

11. Ibid.

12. Ibid.

13. R. I. Holcombe, *History of Marion County Missouri 1884,* reprinted for the Marion County Historical Society (Marceline, Mo.: Walsworth, 1979).

14. *Autobiography.*

15. "The Facts Concerning the Recent Carnival of Crime in Connecticut," in *The Complete Humorous Sketches and Tales of Mark Twain*, edited by Charles Neider (Garden City, N.Y.: Hanover House, 1961).

16. Wecter, op. cit.

17. "Jane Lampton Clemens," included by Paine in *Autobiography.*

18. *Autobiography.*

19. Ibid.

20. *Mark Twain–Howells Letters* (this letter was written May 19, 1886).

21. See footnote p.568 in *Mark Twain–Howells Letters.*

22. Details of these Kentucky and Tennessee years, and of the Clemens family's migration from Tennessee to Florida, Mo., are taken principally from Wecter, op. cit.

23. Mark Twain and Charles Dudley Warner, *The Gilded Age: A Tale of Today* (New York and Oxford, UK: Oxford University Press, 1996).

Chapter 3

1. From a description of a massacre in Minnesota retold by Satan in *Letters from the Earth.*

2. Wecter, op. cit.

3. Ibid.

4. *Autobiography.*

5. Ibid.

6. Ibid.

7. "Chapters from My Autobiography," *The North American Review* (March 1907).

8. In the preface to "Sociable Jimmy," in *Mark Twain: Tales, Speeches, Essays, and Sketches,* edited by Tom Quirk (New York: Penguin, 1994).

9. Ibid.

10. Bernard DeVoto, *Mark Twain's America* (Boston: Little, Brown, 1932).

11. Wecter, op. cit.

12. Ibid.

13. Ibid.

14. DeVoto, *Mark Twain's America.*

15. Ibid.

16. Probably Mrs. T. B. Aldrich in "Crowding Memories," cited by Kaplan, *Mr. Clemens and Mark Twain.*

17. Ibid.

18. Bernard DeVoto, *Mark Twain at Work* (Cambridge, Mass.: Harvard University Press, 1942).

19. Wecter, op. cit.

Chapter 4

1. Wecter, op. cit.

2. Ibid.

3. *Courier-Post* interview.

4. Autobiographical sketch, Berg Collection, New York Public Library; cited by Wecter, op. cit.

5. *The Gilded Age.*

6. *The Galaxy,* quoted by Wecter, op. cit.

7. Van Wyck Brooks, *The Ordeal of Mark Twain* (New York: Dutton, 1920).

8. Letter to the *Philadelphia American Courier,* cited by Everett Emerson, *The Authentic Mark Twain* (Philadelphia: University of Pennsylvania Press, 1984).

9. *Autobiography.*

10. Ibid.

Chapter 5

1. DeVoto, *Mark Twain's America.*

2. Ludwig Lewisohn, *Expression in America* (New York: Harper & Bros., 1932).

3. *Autobiography.*

4. Ibid.

5. *Adventures of Huckleberry Finn* (New York: Random House, 1996).

6. *Autobiography.*

7. Ibid.

8. Ibid.

9. Ibid.

10. Ibid.

11. Letter to the British psychologist John Adams, cited by Kaplan, *Mr. Clemens and Mark Twain.*

12. *Autobiography.*

13. Albert Bigelow Paine, *Mark Twain: A Biography* (New York: Harper & Bros., 1912).

14. *Autobiography.*

15. Ibid.

16. Ibid.

17. Ibid.

18. Ibid.

19. *The Adventures of Tom Sawyer.*

20. Ibid.

21. Ibid.

22. Ibid.

23. Ibid.

24. Notebook entry, cited by Horst H. Kruse in *Mark Twain and Life on the Mississippi* (Boston: University of Massachusetts Press, 1981).

Chapter 6

1. Blair, op. cit.

2. Paine, *Mark Twain: A Biography.*

3. *The Innocents Abroad.*

4. Wecter, op. cit.

5. *Autobiography.*

6. Ibid.

7. Ibid.

8. Ibid.

9. Ibid.

10. Ibid.

11. Ibid.

12. Ibid.

13. Theodore Hornberger, ed., *Mark Twain's Letters to Will Bowen* (Austin: University of Texas, 1941); cited by Kaplan, *Mr. Clemens and Mark Twain.*

14. James M. Cox, *Mark Twain: The Fate of Humor* (Princeton: Princeton University Press, 1966).

15. Mark Twain's letters to Bowen, cited by Wecter, op. cit.; and by Kaplan, *Mr. Clemens and Mark Twain*. Twain revised and softened this draft of a letter he eventually sent to Bowen.

16. Twain's Notebook No. 16, cited by Blair, op. cit.

17. Wecter, op. cit.

18. *Autobiography.*

19. Ibid.

20. Ibid.

21. Interview in the Hannibal *Courier-Post,* April 21, 1910; cited by Wecter, op. cit.

22. Alan Gribben, *Mark Twain's Library: A Reconstruction* (Boston: G. K. Hall, 1980).

23. *Letters from the Earth.*

24. Newspaper clipping; cited by Wecter, op. cit.

25. Letter in the Keokuk *Gate City* in 1862; cited by Emerson, op. cit.

26. Cited by Kaplan, *Mr. Clemens and Mark Twain.*

27. Cited by Emerson, op. cit.

Chapter 7

1. In "The Adventures of Tom Sawyer: A Nightmare Vision of American Boyhood," *Massachusetts Review* (Winter 1980); reprinted in Harold Bloom, ed., *Mark Twain: Modern Critical Views* (New York: Chelsea House, 1986).

2. *Adventures of Huckleberry Finn.*

3. *Autobiography.*

4. Ibid.

5. *The Innocents Abroad.*

6. Ibid.

7. Ibid.

8. *Autobiography.*

9. *Autobiography.*

10. Walt Whitman, *Leaves of Grass* (New York: Penguin Books, 1975).

11. Ben Hecht, *A Child of the Century* (New York: Primus/Donald I. Fine, 1985).

12. *Autobiography*.

13. Paine, *Mark Twain: A Biography*.

14. Wecter, op. cit.

15. *Adventures of Huckleberry Finn: The Only Comprehensive Edition*, Foreword and Addendum by Victor Doyno (New York: Random House, 1996).

16. Ibid.

17. Ibid.

18. Robert Penn Warren, "Mark Twain," *The Southern Review* (July 1972); reprinted in Bloom, op cit.

19. *Adventures of Huckleberry Finn*.

Chapter 8

1. Wecter, op. cit.

2. Paine, *Mark Twain: A Biography*.

3. "Villagers of 1840–3," printed in *Mark Twain's Hannibal, Huck & Tom*.

4. From his afterword to *The Tragedy of Pudd'nhead Wilson* in *The Oxford Mark Twain* (Oxford, UK: Oxford University Press, 1996).

5. *Autobiography*.

6. Wecter, op. cit.

7. Mark Twain papers; cited by Wecter, op cit.

8. Ibid.

9. Wecter, op. cit.

10. Ibid.

11. Kaplan, *Mr. Clemens and Mark Twain*.

12. "Villagers."

13. Ibid.

14. Paine, *Mark Twain: A Biography*.

15. Ibid.

16. Ibid.

17. Brooks, op. cit.

18. Ibid.

29. Ibid.

20. "Life in Letters of William Dean Howells"; cited by Wecter, op. cit.

Chapter 9

1. DeVoto, *Mark Twain's America.*

2. *Life on the Mississippi.*

3. Kenneth S. Lynn, *Mark Twain and Southwestern Humor* (Boston: Atlantic Monthly Press, 1959).

4. Charles William Janson, quoted by Elliott J. Gorn in *American Historical Review,* 90:1 (February 1985).

5. Quoted by Gorn, op cit.

6. Ibid.

7. As heard in the documentary film, *When We Were Kings,* directed by Leon Gast, released in 1996.

8. *Life on the Mississippi.*

9. Lynn, op. cit.

10. Henry B. Wonham, *Mark Twain and the Art of the Tall Tale* (New York: Oxford University Press, 1993).

11. Ibid.

12. Lynn, op. cit.

13. M. H. Dunlop, *Sixty Miles from Contentment* (New York: Basic Books, 1995).

14. Harriet Martineau, quoted by Dunlop, op cit.

15. Timothy Flint, in a letter cited by Gorn, op. cit.

16. Ibid.

17. Lynn, op. cit.

18. Ibid.

19. Ibid.

20. *Life on the Mississippi.*

21. Ibid.

22. From A. B. Longstreet's "Georgia Theatrics," cited by Lynn, op. cit.

23. Lynn, op cit.

24. DeVoto, *Mark Twain's America.*

25. Richard Bucci, "Afterword" to *The Celebrated Jumping Frog of Calaveras County, and Other Sketches,* in *The Oxford Mark Twain.*

26. Cited by Lynn, op. cit.

Chapter 10

1. Michael Schudson, *Discovering the News* (New York: Basic Books, 1978).

2. J. Hurley and Roberta Hagood, *The Story of Hannibal: A Bicentennial History, 1976* (Hannibal, Mo.: The Hannibal Free Public Library [Standard Printing Co.], 1976).

3. *Autobiography.*

4. Cited by Wecter, op. cit.

5. Ibid.

6. *Autobiography.*

7. "William Dean Howells," in *Mark Twain: Tales, Speeches, Essays, and Sketches.*

8. "The Art of Composition," in *Mark Twain: Tales, Speeches, Essays, and Sketches.*

9. Notebook.

10. "The Last Words of Great Men," in *The Curious Republic of Gondour and Other Whimsical Sketches* (New York: Boni & Liveright, 1919).

11. Introduction, in Albert Bigelow Paine, ed., *Mark Twain's Speeches* (New York: Harper, 1910).

12. *Autobiography.*

13. Ibid.

14. Ibid.

15. Ibid.

16. Ibid.

17. Ibid.

18. Ibid.

19. Ibid.

20. Paine, *Mark Twain: A Biography.*

Chapter 11

1. As reprinted in *The Works of Mark Twain: Early Tales & Sketches, Volume 1, 1851–1864,* edited by Edgar Marquess Branch and Robert H. Hirst, with the assistance of Harriet Elinor Smith (Berkeley: University of California Press, 1979).

2. Ibid.

3. Ibid.

4. Jane Clemens letter printed in Samuel C. Webster, ed., *Mark Twain, Business Man* (Boston: Little, Brown, 1946); cited by Wecter, op. cit.

5. *Autobiography.*

6. Ibid.

7. Mark Twain letter to Howells; cited by Kaplan, *Mr. Clemens and Mark Twain.*

8. Twain, "My First Literary Venture," in Neider, ed., *The Complete Humorous Sketches and Tales.*

9. As recounted in "My First Literary Venture."

10. *Early Tales & Sketches.*

11. Ibid.

12. Ibid.

13. "My First Literary Venture."

14. Quoted by Paul Fatout, *Mark Twain in Virginia City* (Bloomington: University of Indiana Press, 1960).

15. *Autobiography.*

16. *Early Tales & Sketches.*

17. Ibid.

18. S. J. Perelman, "And Thou Beside Me, Yacketing in the Wilderness," from *The Road to Milltown, or Under the Spreading Atrophy* (New York: Simon & Schuster, 1957).

19. Ibid.

20. Ibid.

21. *Autobiography.*

22. *The Adventures of Tom Sawyer.*

23. *Autobiography.*

24. Ibid.

25. Ibid.

26. Ibid.
27. *Early Tales & Sketches.*
28. Wecter, op. cit.
29. Ibid.

Chapter 12

1. *Life on the Mississippi.*
2. Kerouac, *On the Road* (New York: Viking, the 40th Anniversary Edition, 1997).
3. *Life on the Mississippi.*
4. Ibid.
5. Hannibal *Journal;* cited by Wecter, op. cit.
6. *Life on the Mississippi.*
7. *The Adventures of Tom Sawyer.*
8. *Life on the Mississippi.*
9. Ibid.
10. Hagood and Hagood, op. cit.
11. Ibid.
12. Ibid.
13. R. Kent Rasmussen, *Mark Twain A to Z: The Essential Reference to his Life and Writings* (New York: Facts on File, 1995).
14. *Life on the Mississippi.*
15. Cited by Wecter, op. cit.
16. *Early Tales & Sketches.*
17. Ibid.
18. Ibid.
19. Ibid.
20. Ibid.
21. Paine, *Mark Twain: A Biography.*
22. *Roughing It.*
23. Wecter, op. cit.
24. *Early Tales & Sketches.*
25. Ibid.
26. Wecter., op. cit.

27. DeLancy Ferguson, *Mark Twain: Man and Legend* (New York Charter Books, 1963).
28. Paine, *Mark Twain: A Biography.*
29. *Autobiography.*

Chapter 13

1. *Mark Twain's Letters, Volume 1: 1853–1866,* edited by Edgar Marquess Branch, Michael B. Frank, and Kenneth M. Sanderson (Berkeley: University of California Press, 1988).
2. Jay Parini, *John Steinbeck: A Biography* (New York: Holt, 1995).
3. *Mark Twain's Letters, Vol. 1.*
4. Ibid.
5. Ibid.
6. Ibid.
7. Ibid.
8. Ibid.
9. Ibid.
10. Ibid.
11. Ibid.
12. Ibid.
13. Ibid.
14. Ibid.
15. Ibid.
16. Ibid.
17. Ibid.
18. Ibid.

Chapter 14

1. Paine, *Mark Twain: A Biography.*
2. *Autobiography.*
3. Ibid.
4. Margaret Sanborn, *Mark Twain: The Bachelor Years* (New York: Doubleday, 1990).

5. From Orion Clemens's unpublished autobiography, cited by Paine, *Mark Twain: A Biography.*

6. Cited in *Mark Twain's Letters, Vol. 1.*

7. Paine, *Mark Twain: A Biography.*

8. Sanborn, op. cit.

9. Cited in *Mark Twain's Letters, Vol. 1.*

10. Sanborn, op. cit.

11. Ibid.

12. In "The Turning Point of My Life," *Harper's Bazaar* (February 1910).

13. From William Lewis Herndon and Lardner Gibbon, *Exploration of the Valley of the Amazon, Made Under Direction of the Navy Department* (1853–54); cited in *Mark Twain's Letters, Vol. 1.*

14. "Another Grand Filibuster Scheme!" *Daily St. Louis Intelligencer,* March 15, 1855; cited by Edgar Marquess Branch, Mark Twain's Letters, vol. 1, 1853–1866 (Berkeley: University of California Press, 1988).

15. Ibid.

16. Cited by Paine, *Mark Twain: A Biography.*

17. *Mark Twain's Letters, Vol. 1.*

18. Ibid.

19. Ibid.

20. From "Puddn'head Wilson's New Calendar" in "Following the Equator." New York: Oxford University Press, 1996.

21. Cited in Sanborn, op. cit.

22. Ibid.

23. Ibid.

24. *Life on the Mississippi.*

25. Ibid.

26. Ibid.

27. Ibid.

28. Paine, *Mark Twain: A Biography.*

29. Ibid.

30. Ibid.

31. Ibid.

32. Ibid.

33. Mark Twain's autobiographical notes, cited in *Mark Twain's Letters, Vol. 1.*

34. *Life on the Mississippi.*
35. Ibid.
36. Ibid.

Chapter 15

1. Richard Bridgman, *Traveling in Mark Twain* (Berkeley: University of California Press, 1987).
2. *Life on the Mississippi.*
3. Ibid.
4. DeVoto, *Mark Twain's America.*
5. From the New Orleans *True American,* May 11, 1837; cited in Louis C. Hunter, *Steamboats on the Western Rivers* (Boston: Harvard University Press, 1949).
6. Ibid.
7. Ibid.
8. *Life on the Mississippi.*
9. Ibid.
10. Ibid.
11. Paine, *Mark Twain: A Biography.*
12. *Life on the Mississippi.*

Chapter 16

1. *Mark Twain's Letters, Vol. 1.*
2. *Life on the Mississippi.*
3. Ibid.
4. "River News," the Pittsburgh *Gazette,* February 15, 1854; cited in *Mark Twain's Letters, Vol. 1.*
5. Information regarding Clemens's activities in this period is summarized in *Mark Twain's Letters, Vol. 1.*
6. Ibid.
7. Ibid.
8. *Life on the Mississippi.*
9. *Autobiography.*

10. Ibid.

11. Ibid.

12. Ibid.

13. John Lauber, *The Making of Mark Twain* (New York: American Heritage, 1985).

14. *Autobiography.*

15. Ibid.

16. From Pascal Covici, Jr., "Dear Master Wattie: The Mark Twain–David Watt Bowser Letters," *The Southwest Review* (Spring 1960); cited in Kaplan, *Mr. Clemens and Mark Twain.*

17. *Autobiography.*

18. Ibid.

19. Ibid.

20. Ibid.

21. *Life on the Mississippi.*

22. *Mark Twain's Notebooks and Journals, Volume 1 (1855–1873),* edited by Frederick Anderson, Michael B. Frank, and Kenneth M. Sanderson; *The Mark Twain Papers* (Berkeley: University of California Press, 1975).

23. *Life on the Mississippi.*

24. Ibid.

25. Ibid.

26. Ibid.

27. Ibid.

28. Ibid.

29. Ibid.

30. Ibid.

31. *Mark Twain's Letters, Vol. 1.*

32. *Life on the Mississippi.*

33. Ibid.

34. "The Disaster to the Steamer Pennsylvania: Statement of an Eyewitness," in the Memphis *Morning Bulletin,* June 22, 1858; cited in *Mark Twain's Letters, Vol. 1.*

35. Ibid.

36. *Life on the Mississippi.*

37. Letter to Mollie Clemens, June 18, 1858; cited in *Mark Twain's Letters, Vol. 1.*

38. Fragment of an undated newspaper article; cited in *Mark Twain's Letters, Vol. 1.*

39. *Mark Twain's Letters, Vol. 1.*

40. Ibid.

41. From "Pudd'nhead Wilson's Calendar" in *Pudd'nhead Wilson,* written in 1894.

42. *Mark Twain's Letters, Vol. 1.*

43. *Autobiography.*

44. Ibid.

Chapter 17

1. St. Louis *Post-Dispatch,* May 30, 1902.

2. Ibid.

3. Ibid.

4. Ibid.

5. Ibid.

6. Ibid.

7. Ibid.

8. Ibid.

INDEX

Index

Index

Index